Becoming Essential

**For associations, the question is:
Do you want to survive, or do you want to thrive?**

By James E. Meyers

About the author

James E. Meyers founded Chicago-based Imagination in 1994. Imagination has transitioned over its 25-year history from being a leader in custom publishing to being recognized today as one of the top content marketing agencies in America, including being named Content Marketing Agency of the Year in 2012 and ranked one of the top 21 most creative content marketing agencies in 2014 and 2016. Jim was named Custom Media Innovator of the Year in 2009 by American Business Media, and was awarded the Mitch Mohanna Lifetime Achievement Award by Association Media & Publishing in 2019.

Prior to Imagination, Jim was the group president of Macmillan Business Publishing for five years. He also served as senior vice president of marketing for the Chicago Sun-Times. Jim received a bachelor's degree in marketing and advertising from the Indiana University School of Business. He also completed an Advanced Advertising Management program at Northwestern University and the Darden Business School's Leadership Program at the University of Virginia.

Join the conversation on Twitter @jmeyers or visit our website: www.becoming-essential.com.

Acknowledgments

Since founding Imagination 25 years ago, I have had the privilege of working with a number of great association leaders. During that time, as the internet and social media have exploded, many of those leaders have faced dramatic changes and threats to their historic reason for existence.

In the face of change, I've seen it go both ways: Some associations have begun to transform their business models to become more essential than ever before. Others are still struggling to adapt.

That's why I decided 18 months ago to write a book that might help associations see the way forward. Knowing I couldn't do it alone, I enlisted the help of some of the best strategic thinkers and journalists I know to help me brainstorm and write *Becoming Essential*.

First, I'd like to thank Simona Covel, my writing partner. Simona's deep journalistic experience as a business editor and writer was invaluable in converting hours of rambling ideas about how associations could survive and thrive into a cohesive, clear and beautifully written book.

I'd also like to thank Imagineers Kim Caviness and Rebecca Rolfes for their subject matter research and editorial contributions. Deep thanks and credit also go to Doug Kelly, who has led the Imagination design team since our beginning, for creating a clean and compelling design for the book. And Connie Otto and Amy Fabbri at Imagination provided the production guidance and project management that we all needed to stay on track.

Sincere thanks go to the more than 20 association leaders and thinkers who agreed to be interviewed for this book. Their firsthand lessons are essential for allowing others to carve a path forward.

Finally, I'd like to thank my wife, Bonnie, and my three daughters, who have made the sacrifices over the past 25 years that have allowed me to achieve my dream of creating a world-class content marketing agency.

Contents

Introdu

ction

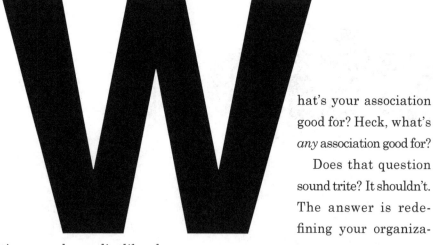

hat's your association good for? Heck, what's *any* association good for?

Does that question sound trite? It shouldn't. The answer is redefining your organizations—and your livelihoods.

Most of you, if asked what your association or any association is good for, will come up with a pretty consistent answer, something along the lines of: content, community, career development. That answer has remained remarkably unchanged for the last 30, 40, even 50 years.

In 2016 (the last year the data is available), the IRS recognized nearly 64,000 trade and professional associations.[1] Sixty-four thousand trade and professional associations, all providing some form of content, community and career development. Associations represent everyone from dog walkers to scientists to window washers. Can they all survive—or, even better, thrive? Probably not. The future is closing in, and many associations find themselves in an existential vise, unsure of a path forward.

Most associations long ago started dealing with the obvious threats. You've known for years that certain tactical changes had to be made. As a result, the delivery of your content, your education and your networking has changed. You have a nice website. Your content is digital and available in multiple formats. You offer webinars and online networking opportunities. But is that enough? Has your organization shifted in the same way that the world has shifted?

Be honest: Under the surface, how different does your association look from the one your predecessor, or your predecessor's predecessor, ran?

For many associations, the answer is: not different enough. That's why so many associations are caught in a continual, self-defeating cycle of catch-up, trying to identify and capitalize on the latest trends in the delivery of education or content. Which associations will thrive? Not the ones that simply create some digital content, plan webinars and hold an annual conference. The paradigm has shifted. That doesn't mean that the value proposition has changed; most likely, it hasn't. Most likely, your association provides those same foundational supports—content, community and career development—but the *way* you provide them has to change. And I'm not just talking about the channels where you're delivering them.

What I'm talking about is making yourself essential. You can work feverishly, day and night, to improve your members' lives. You can provide them with seamless professional development opportunities, rich forums for networking and tons of cutting-edge knowledge. Today, that's no longer enough. They can turn elsewhere for education. They have other sources of content and networking.

To thrive, you have to shift how we think about the fundamental role of an association. We've all watched over the last decade as associations reacted, shifted or pivoted in response to the Great Recession and the blow it dealt. Some associations quickly changed course to become more global, courting international members to offset any economic softening at home. Others decided membership was obsolete and shored up a collection of variously priced products and services.

None of that matters if your members don't find your organization compelling. Your products and services can be top-notch, your membership pricing structure clear and reasonable, your educational offerings helpful. It won't matter if members and prospective members aren't drawn to you. You still need to provide content, connections and career development—but the meaning of those things has changed.

You need product value and brand value. You need your members to think about you as providing an essential service, one they are unwilling to do without. This is no different for associations than it is for any other industry: Tesla could make the best electric car in the world, but if it looked like a run-of-the-mill, inelegant steel box on wheels, no one would buy it.

Other industries and sectors got used to this dynamic a long time ago. After all, it was Henry Ford who said that his customers could have any color Model T they wanted—as long as it was black. That was fine when Ford was the only game in town. But that ethos didn't last long in the auto industry as competition heated up over the course of the 20th century. Today, automakers are falling all over themselves to compete with Tesla and its ilk.

That dynamic has finally landed in the world of associations. Even in tough times, you used to skate by because of member loyalty—or was it obligation?—but now your lives have changed. Loyalty, says one of the association executive directors I talked to for this book, used to disguise the weakness in associations. No longer.

Today, it's not enough to work on behalf of your members—the mandate you try to live up to every day, every month, every year. You still have to provide that core value every day, all the time, innovating as the market changes. But maybe more importantly, you have to *prove* your relevance, to both your members and, often, the public.

That's new territory for associations. How do you prove it? I'm about to tell you. Let's get started.

Part I
Disrupt

ion

What Are Your Disruptors?

"We're trying to transform our organization. Not just in terms of business model—but to what creates and delivers value." —Scott Wiley, president and CEO, the Ohio Society of CPAs

isruptions eventually pummel just about every industry. The telegram was disrupted by the telephone. The horse-drawn buggy was disrupted by the car. In recent years, brick and mortar retail was disrupted by e-commerce. As the disruptors gain steam, what differentiates the businesses that drift into oblivion (goodbye, Kmart) from those that thrive (hello, Target)?

The answers are complicated and vary across industries, but they always have something in common: acceptance of what's changing and the willingness to make concerted, real changes to adapt to a new environment. It's not happenstance that Target has thrived while Kmart faded away. As Walmart and Amazon encroached, Kmart essentially did the same things it always had: focused on mass-market, non-differentiated products sold through retail stores. That meant that as the market changed around it, it was forced to continually liquidate assets in a race to remain solvent. Target? It changed course. It intensified marketing and the differentiating focus on its "Tar-zhay" image, while acknowledging the inevitable move toward digital and intensifying its focus on speedy delivery and ease of ordering.

In short: One recognized that the future of retail would look very different and pivoted accordingly, carving out a role that competed with the marketplace but found the white space within it. The other has been caught in a deadly reactionary cycle, letting stores fall into disarray and then ultimately closing locations to try to stay solvent as customers abandon the brand.

When it comes to facing the future of their business model, associations aren't as different from other industries as you might like to think. Associations are being pummeled with a series of disruptions that have changed the way they think and operate. The world has changed. No longer do people enter a profession, join an association or society as a matter of course and remain a member for decades. Instead, joining an association is something optional, something that professionals will do only if they perceive true, tangible value. This we know. But why, and what are you doing about it?

Disruptor No. 1: Technology

I'll start with the disruptor we've all been grappling with for years. It's been nearly 20 years since association leaders started wringing their hands about the shifting technological landscape and what it would portend for them.

A few of the reasons for technology's blow are fairly obvious—and not particularly new. All it takes to realize the change that tech has wrought is to think back to the three core values that associations classically bring: content, connection and career development. In each case, the classic model of association value has long ago been upended.

I won't spend lots of time dwelling on this, since you live and breathe it every day. But to be clear about some of the big changes for those bread and butter services:

- **Content:** Remember when the member magazine was the be-all, end-all of association communications? Members routinely cited the magazine as one of the top two or three benefits of association membership. That magazine—and maybe a few other periodic forms of printed communication—was the main means for members to receive industry updates and information on what peers were doing.

- **Connection:** The trade show or annual conference was a yearly revelation. It served as a reunion, a meetup, a social center, an education hub. Companies sent a dozen or more employees at a time. Attendees eagerly awaited the high-profile speakers and the opportunity to compare notes and network with peers.
- **Career development:** Associations were the gatekeepers for learning, providing unparalleled opportunities for courses and certification. Plus, that annual trade show was unmatched in allowing people to connect and look for their next opportunity.

When associations were founded, and through the end of the 20th century, there was no LinkedIn. There were no Facebook groups, no virtually arranged meetups. Workers long relied on association meetings to network with colleagues near and far, to glean new knowledge and to see where their profession was heading.

Today, the foundation of the association has been shaken. While most association leaders would argue that the role of the association is still rooted in content, community and career development, those core competencies must be considered through a much broader lens (more on this later) and delivered in vastly different ways. "The value proposition is the same," says Kevin Marvel, executive officer of the American Astronomical Society (AAS). "It's a way of getting together with others who share the same research, interests, etc. The difference is the channels. We evolve not as much our value proposition as the way we engage with people who want that value proposition."

Disruptor No. 2: Economics

We all have what feels like a thousand things vying for our eyes and our brainpower at every moment. With every passing year, the competition for attention—sometimes called the attention economy—becomes fiercer.

One of the first books about the attention economy was written in 2001, just as people were really beginning to grapple with the idea of an always-on system of information delivery. The authors, two Accenture consultants and researchers, open the book with an anecdote bemoaning a professional workplace where the employees "resort to instant messages because regular emails aren't attention-getting enough. Even commutes are consumed by cellphone conversations or voicemail." It's all designed to sound overwhelming and shocking.

Living in today's world, it's hard to imagine a time when all you had competing for your attention were phone calls, emails and IMs—it sounds positively quaint!

Instead, today's professionals—and everyone else—grapple with a constant onslaught of distractions: emails, calls and IMs, sure, but also a never-ending stream of social media, incessant news updates and the siren call of whatever always-on apps we might have downloaded on our phones and tablets.

Yes, it's only gotten worse in the nearly two decades since *The Attention Economy* was written. And that has very real implications for associations. If yours was the only e-newsletter your members received, chances are they'd read it, from beginning to end. If you were the only Facebook group they belonged to, they'd be in there, posting and commenting. But you're just one of dozens competing for time and attention.

Indeed, attention has become currency. Think of how much more online ads cost when they get clicked on. Consider the perceived value to a marketer of a "like" or social media comment. That's all a reflection of just how desperate we've become for consumer attention.

The companies and organizations sending messages into the abyss aren't the only ones who are desperate. So too are all of us who are trying to manage information overload day in and day out.

That's why an entire discipline has grown up helping people navigate their phones and laptops. So now we don't just have dozens of books for CEOs and marketers about how to handle the attention economy, but we also have books for your average Joe on how to handle it. The research on the topic spans business, psychology and education: It's an affliction with virtually no bounds. To combat it, there are books like *Don't Miss Your Life: Find More Joy and Fulfillment Now*, which is an actual how-to guide about managing the constant barrage of information. Then there's *A Field Guide to Lies: Critical Thinking in the Information Age*, a book that gives you tips for things like "understanding the hierarchies of source quality and bias that distort the information we take in—as a skill to guard against information overload," according to a *Fast Company* article.

In other words, as a society, we're having so much trouble managing the endless information coming at us all day, every day, that we need even more information to teach us to wade through all of the information in a productive way. We simply can't handle it—we're unable to reap what we've sowed.

21st-Century Problem: Infobesity

No one knows what to do with all of the information they signed up for. We even have a new word for it: infobesity. That's right, we're so overloaded on information that we're bloated and unhealthy.

One British psychologist, Glenn Wilson, coined the word "info-mania"[2] to describe the crazed reaction the brain has to trying to volley from one task to another. Trying to concentrate on a task when there's an unread email sitting in your inbox, Wilson says, lops 10 points off your effective IQ.[3]

The antidote to infobesity? Many practitioners recommend information diets.

Where does that leave those of us running associations? You've probably already heard that the human attention span, at eight seconds, is now shorter than a goldfish's.[4] Whether that's true or not (I have my

Takeaway: When it comes to content, the same tactics you employed 10 or five or even three years ago are unlikely to work.

doubts), suffice it to say that if you're competing with 72 other emailers in your members' inboxes on any given morning, it's hard to stand out. The same tactics you employed 10 or five or even three years ago are unlikely to work. The last thing you want is to contribute to infobesity with a deluge of subpar content. That will endear you to no one.

On top of the attention economy, we're all also grappling with what I'll call the compression economy—that is, the idea that everyone is trying to do more for less. It's been a decade since the Great Recession clamped down on corporate spending. But even as the recovery churns on, the profligate spending has not returned. In many industries, there's a "new normal," where company-funded travel and spending on extras are simply no longer in the cards. It's about productivity, productivity, productivity.

That's largely because during the slow, sluggish economic recovery, many businesses learned to get by with less—they learned that it was possible, after all, to operate with fewer people, less stuff, less spending. At one point in 2010, as the economy was beginning to show gains again, CNN reported that gross domestic product had recovered 84 percent of the output that was lost during the recession, but the labor market had recouped only 11 percent of the jobs that were lost.[5] That pattern continued for years, as even the biggest companies re-stuffed their coffers rather than hiring and spending.

While hiring eventually picked up, driving the unemployment rate down to near historical lows, the ethos of doing more for less stuck around. The compression economy isn't just about doing more with less money. It's about doing more with less money, less time, less training. The new world of business moves faster every day, and we're all trying to figure out how to keep up. That means that even if the money's not an issue, companies are less likely to allow staff to take four days off for a conference or spend on multiple memberships and subscriptions. No one wants to be labeled wasteful or to be seen as the person who engenders corporate bloat.

And while I obviously don't believe that associations should be put in the bloat category, I do think they have an image problem. The issue isn't what associations provide every day, which continues to be incredibly valuable for hundreds of thousands of people. It's about making everyone—even those you don't think of as your audience—aware of just how valuable you are. That's where many associations fall down. As the AAS's Marvel noted, the value proposition is the same. But how you deliver that value proposition has to change. I would argue that how you telegraph it has to change, too. More on that in Chapter 2.

Disruptor No. 3: Culture

Some of the pressures facing associations can't simply be tied to evolving technologies or the sort of creative disruption that has faced countless industries since the horse-drawn carriage business folded in the face of the Model T.

The core of the idea of an association is the word "associate"—the implicit idea of a connection to something. What happens when the very idea of what constitutes an "association" with something begins to change?

At the broadest level, that's a societal shift—a global one, really—that professional and trade associations need to contend with. And that's the shift that has begun chipping away at thousands of associations.

Many associations used to take their membership for granted. The pattern for members was simply: graduate, join association, renew every year. For most associations, that's simply no longer true. And that's a reflection of something more than just a population of people connecting on LinkedIn and Twitter. That's a reflection of a change in the way people view community and connections.

Much has been said and written about the rise of identity politics. This isn't a book about politics, and I definitely don't want to go there.

We're in the world of "you do you." What comes with that is less adherence to group norms and a great rise of individual emphasis.

But if art imitates life, so too does politics. Today's society is much more focused on the individual than ever before. We're in the world of "you do you." What comes with that is less adherence to group norms and a great rise of individual emphasis.

That shift has implications for associations. In his recent book *The Fractured Republic*, author Yuval Levin argues that in part, that individualism has led Americans to become less strictly adhered to tight networks. Instead, our networks are broader, more diffuse. You're probably thinking about social media, and rightfully so. But Levin says that technology—social platforms like LinkedIn—are examples of that; they're not the cause. Rather, those tech-enabled vast networks have emerged as Americans have become less beholden to small, tightly knit groups.

That may mean, then, that your members are simply less beholden to you. They may be less likely to automatically renew each year, less likely to see writing that annual check as something they just have to do. Much has been written and said about the move away from loyalty. Not everyone agrees that loyalty is dead, but certain trend lines are unmistakable. There's no question that employees view their contract with their employers differently than they used to. Gone are the days of 30 years at one company, followed by a retirement party and a gold watch. And with good reason. Pensions have largely gone the way of tube TVs, leaving workers responsible for their own retirement savings. Benefits ebb when the economy sinks—a far cry from the halcyon days of paternalistic companies like Kodak, which once dominated employment in Rochester, New York, with its employee bowling alley, traveling nurses and visiting symphony.[6] Company towns are all but dead, and so is lifetime employment.

Corporate culture has changed, bringing instead a shift to an unrelenting emphasis on shareholder value. Employees haven't always been averse to this. In fact, a lot of us are more invested in shareholder value than ever: The rise of 401(k)s for retirement saving—and the demise of pensions—means that for the first time in history, a critical mass of Americans have their fates tied to the stock market. That means

Employers are less paternalistic

Employees are less likely to spend decades at a single company

Workers become more focused on individualism

Workers focus on what's in it for them

They become less loyal to a single entity

that maximizing shareholder value is, theoretically, in *everyone's* best interest.

But is it, really? This idea, that it's better to consider the bottom line than to lavish employees with benefits, has been around for a while now. And, while no one was really paying attention, it has had a cascading effect over the last 50 years.

What does this have to do with associations? Bear with me; I'm almost there. When companies cut costs, when they don't invest in workers, workers are less likely to stick around. When workers are less likely to stick around at a single company, they become more focused on their own individualism. That sense of me-first permeates everything: The idea that you are responsible for your professional ascent and your financial well-being. The individual becomes more important than any group, business or organization. Workers simply aren't going to stick around because it's "the right thing to do" or the way things have always been done.

"We've tended over the years to just assume that members will just want to belong," says Robert Harington, associate executive director for publishing at the American Mathematical Society. Today, he says, the mindset has shifted. "What's in it for them? That's the question. It's difficult."

The move away from automatic joining and loyalty has tremendous implications. For one, it means that other organizations or companies are free to encroach on what's traditionally been your territory—and members and prospective members will simply follow their favorite offerings, wherever they're being offered. That may be LinkedIn, or it may be some other organization or company: Two-thirds of professional association members (67 percent) have used a for-profit company for an activity traditionally provided by an association, according to 2016 research from Rockbridge.[7]

Consider conferences, says Bob Weidner, president and CEO of the Metals Service Center Institute (MSCI), a trade association. MSCI has as many as three or four competitors for its conference business—and none of them are trade associations. Those for-profit, nonmembership-based

Takeaway: Associations' most vulnerable business? Networking.

organizations may offer wider access or lower rates because of their business model. They "play by a different set of rules," Weidner says.

What's associations' most vulnerable area? Networking, according to Rockbridge. That's right, networking: one of associations' bulwarks. Nearly a quarter (23 percent) of the association members Rockbridge surveyed believe for-profit companies do it better, and 38 percent believe they do it equally well.

Who those companies are will vary across verticals and sectors. Think: MarketingProfs for marketing industry professionals or Doximity for physicians. Whoever they are, you'd better know the companies that are offering networking for your members and understand the potential threat they represent to you.

But the end of loyalty also has potential positive implications for associations. After all, if more workers than ever are relentlessly focused on their own advancement, shouldn't they be more likely to need the services of a professional association?

Yes. But you can't speak to them as you always have or about what you traditionally have. Again, it comes back not necessarily to the value proposition itself, but the way you deliver it.

Disruptor No. 4: The Expectations of Your Members

You've always had a purpose: to further your members' careers and industries. It's a great purpose, a binding, driving purpose that has driven thousands of associations, some of them for hundreds of years.

But here's the bad news: Acting out that purpose the way you're used to is no longer enough. Your members want more. Your members—especially those in the early part of their career—view their profession as inextricably linked to their life out of work. They might be scientists or marketers or physicians or closet organizers. Whoever they are, their professional life and their personal life have likely merged. This is the Instagram world: a generation of people for whom branding themselves is second nature. Whatever their chosen profession, it's part of who they

Takeaway: Associations have a much larger mandate than ever before.

are. They don't turn work off when they leave the office each day. They don't compartmentalize.

"It seems like the current generation has a much more comprehensive view of the world," says the AAS's Marvel. "They expect their professional society to be supportive of them in ways that aren't just supportive of them in their professions, but as people."

This is huge. It means that associations have a much larger mandate than ever before. It means that furthering your members' careers and their professions is a broader issue than it ever has been, one that's wrapped up in public perception and sociopolitical issues.

Marvel has experienced this firsthand. In 2016, a group of younger AAS members grew increasingly troubled by reports of U.S. police violence against African-Americans. The group sent a proposal to the organization suggesting that the AAS should weigh in publicly on the issue.

"They expect their professional society to be supportive of them in ways that aren't just supportive of them in their professions, but as people."

To them, there was a direct connection between this pressing societal issue and their association: They believed, Marvel says, that speaking out was the AAS's rightful role, that it was incumbent upon a professional society to clearly state that it supports all minorities in science.

"Our older members kind of couldn't get their head around it," Marvel remembers. "Why would we weigh in on something when it's not directly connected to professional research?" But on the other hand, Marvel says, he and the board were keenly aware that if you were a young African-American astronomer or an African-American graduate student pursuing astronomy, these issues would be dominating your day and your thoughts and potentially affecting your work. Maybe, they thought, it's incumbent upon a professional society to support its members as they pursue their work—even if the link isn't immediately apparent or direct.

A proposal to speak out on the issue was submitted by the member group to the AAS board of directors. The board quickly convened a committee to debate the issue. Should they stay silent? Come down on one side or the other of the politically heated topic? After some debate, with the help of one of the young scientists who had submitted the proposal, they ended up drafting a statement that landed in the middle ground. It offered broad-based support for minorities in scientific fields.

After the statement was issued, Marvel says, the organization received around 20 emails complaining about the content, some griping that it had no business going there, others saying the statement didn't go far enough.

If you haven't found yourself here yet, embroiled in a politically charged conversation about something seemingly afield from the core of the profession you represent, chances are it won't be long. It's part of a bigger-picture shift.

The expectation that association leadership move into these sometimes-uncharted waters reflects the shifting expectations that society has for its leaders. Consider the highly regarded Edelman Trust Barometer. Each year, the international public relations firm employs its proprietary barometer to measure the level of trust that the public holds for a variety of public and private institutions. In the 2018 survey, the United States market showed a 37-point aggregate drop in trust—the largest drop of any country.[8]

This is not a minor thing. Edelman puts it starkly:

"It is no exaggeration to state that the U.S. has reached a point of crisis that should provoke every leader, in government, business, or civil sector, into urgent action. Inertia is not an option, and neither is silence. The public's confidence in the traditional structures of American leadership is now fully undermined and has been replaced with a strong sense of fear, uncertainty and disillusionment."

Takeaway: Fake news benefits credible organizations.

The reasons are many: A historically bitter presidential election left Americans with little trust in politicians and government. An increasingly harsh glare on police violence has chipped away at Americans' trust in law enforcement. The rampant rise of fake news has led to widespread distrust of social media and the information that's disseminated there. According to the survey, fully 63 percent of the U.S. general population has trouble distinguishing what is fake news and what's real. "The public is fearful, and trust is disturbingly low," Edelman notes in the report.[9]

This is bad news. We should all be worried about it. But it also presents an opportunity—a duty, really—for those of us who are leading businesses or organizations. While the public's trust in a number of institutions is faltering, one of the Edelman survey's notable findings was that trust in CEOs is on the rise. Business is trusted more than government, and of all institutions, nongovernmental organizations enjoy the highest level of trust.

On top of that, Edelman survey respondents revealed an expectation that business leaders put themselves out there when it comes to issues that affect their business or their industry: 56 percent of respondents said they "have no respect for CEOs that remain silent on important issues"[10] and a whopping 84 percent said they *expect* CEOs to inform conversations and policy debates around one or more issues across the universe of economic trends, including immigration, health care, global warming and discrimination.

This, too, is huge. What all of that means is that the scenario that played out over Black Lives Matter at the American Astronomical Society is likely to be playing out in all sorts of ways at associations across the country.

Many high-profile for-profit companies are already navigating these waters. Google, with its famously outspoken, politically active employee base, has struggled to control the sometimes-charged political conversations that have come to dominate its California headquarters. For example, when the PETA president was brought to Google headquarters by the group Googlers for Animals, there was opposition by the Black Googler

Network because they were offended that PETA had compared prejudice against animals to racism.[11] The nonstop political debates can dominate conversation and lead to uncomfortable disputes among employees—not to mention sucking up time and energy.

You may be thinking that what goes for Google doesn't exactly go for the rest of the country. After all, Google is notably liberal and has long been known for public statements on hot issues. But these days it's not just hip Silicon Valley companies that are finding themselves in the middle of political conversations.

Look at Walmart. Yes, Walmart—the largest private employer in America, which is not exactly known for activism of any sort. The middle America mainstay is also heading into this heated territory, led by none other than its mild-mannered CEO. The retailer issued a statement raising the gun-purchasing age to 21 following a spate of school shootings. That followed a 2015 incident when the CEO spoke out against an Arkansas bill that would have allowed people to refuse service to customers based on their own religious beliefs.

"There is not a part of me that says, 'That's political. I'd love to get involved in that,'" CEO Doug McMillon explained at a conference. But "society expects things of leading companies, and sometimes we should take a stance on something."

Executives today simply have no choice: Their customers want their purchases to align with their views. CEOs increasingly see telegraphing their social consciousness as part of their mission as company leaders.

"It's no longer a question of if, but where, when and how to engage on these issues and what type of topics to engage on," Lawrence Parnell, associate professor at the strategic public relations program at George Washington University's Graduate School of Political Management, told *The Wall Street Journal*.[12] When do you choose to take a stand, and how much do you worry about alienating customers or clients who may not agree? "These are new challenges and things CEOs and boards never had to deal with before, so they are struggling."

The answer to when to take a stand starts by remembering your mission. I'm not advocating that, as associations, you make a statement on every hot-button social or political issue that comes along. Compared with for-profit companies, associations should have less of a struggle to figure out when to take a stand, and the path to navigate should be much clearer, since you have a much narrower mandate than huge, multinational corporations with customers across every conceivable part of the spectrum. Even so, this is a tough road to walk, without a doubt.

While many trade organizations are comfortable wading into sometimes-charged territory, many professional associations are not. No matter the association, taking a stand in today's acrimonious political climate is not easy. It can lead to some heated conversations, both between leadership and the board, and between leadership and members. That's not all: Depending on the issue, you will probably end up with members who threaten to walk, whether or not they go through with it.

Scott Wiley, the president and CEO of the Ohio Society of CPAs (OSCPA), is quick to note that his organization is not generally involved in social issues. But that doesn't mean the organization can stay out of politics. Plus, he doesn't believe it should. Particularly as the organization's membership has grown younger—it's now two-thirds millennial and Gen Z, a quick flip from two-thirds boomer or older five years ago—the members are simply more socially conscious. Much like Marvel's experience at the AAS, OSCPA members expect the association to support them in the areas where their profession and social causes intersect.

Especially in a state like Ohio, with chronic, deep political divides, that leaves Wiley and the board with a tough tightrope to walk. How do they support the socially conscious leanings of their membership without appearing politicized? When is it appropriate to step in?

For many associations, that comes in knowing your purpose and always being true to it. For most of us, that means carving out a role taking a stance on social issues that are also professional issues—like the astronomers' statement on minorities in science.

How to Take a Stand—Even If You'd Rather Not
Edelman offers CEOs a three-part recommendation to navigate
building trust and leading through charged times.
- Lead with purpose—Declare your purpose, and live it
- Be authentic—Engage on relevant issues and don't hide
  behind corporate speak and platitudes
- Galvanize employees—Know what's important to them, and
  act on it

That will play out differently depending on your association's mission. Wiley looks at it this way: His job, and OSCPA's job, is to "do whatever it takes to advance business in Ohio," because when you bring business to Ohio, you bring a need for CPAs. So, when he was deciding whether to act on issues of LGBTQ inclusion, he thought, "Well, that's not a social issue for us, that's a workplace issue for us," he says. "Why would we want to do anything to prevent talent from wanting to work in our state and from thinking it's a good place to be? It's just good business sense."

To that end, the Ohio Society of CPAs launched a three-year diversity inclusion program focused on bringing more women and minorities into the profession and supporting them once they're there. And like at the AAS, not all members are thrilled. Wiley recounts a recent email from a member who noted that it's one thing to talk about diversity and inclusion; that he was fine with. But he suddenly felt a lot less fine when the association was spending his membership dues on diversity programming.

Comments like that aren't going to slow him down, Wiley says. There's no going back to the time when social issues and business issues didn't overlap. For association execs walking that fine line, "this is the reality of our country, and we've got to lead on. When I get home, do I want to crack open a bottle of wine? Sure. But our job is to make sure we're informing our members with the knowledge they need to be successful."

Wiley sees a secondary benefit to promoting sometimes-controversial programs like diversity and inclusion, too—the opportunity to be seen as a leader in business practices. Already, he's had inquiries from other business groups around the state and country, looking to his organization for information and guidance on how to develop their business and train employees when it comes to diversity and inclusion.

That doesn't mean, Wiley is quick to note, that the association is going to start getting involved in every hot-button political issue or firestorm. Far from it. He knows this is going to come up over and over again, along with all of the attendant debate and discourse—which means the organization needs a specific plan for how to cope.

In deciding which issues to wade into, it's critical to have a decision matrix—a framework for whether to get involved. For Wiley, that comes back to having crystal clarity around what the organization stands for: in his case, making business grow in Ohio. If the issue is relevant to that mission, then they're liable to get involved. If it's not—even if it's something members are passionate about—they're not going there. All along the way, Wiley notes, one of the hardest parts is to be transparent in how the decisions are being made. "People are so passionate about the things they believe—they want the organizations they belong to to have those shared values," he says. "It requires organizations to have clarity around who they are, what they stand for and that for which they will not stand."

It's not easy. The conversations are tough. The nuances are many. Divisiveness is practically guaranteed. But it's the crucial path for associations to thrive in the world today, Wiley believes. "The ones who resist are choosing their own destiny, and it's not a destiny that I think is a strong one," he says.

Disruptor No. 5: External Pressures

The world has always been full of activists and media pressure. But it hasn't always been so public. Trade associations' activities, for one, weren't always so out in the open; they were able to go about lobbying

Your mission

Speak out

Social issue

or other government affairs business pretty quietly. Not so today. Legislative visitor logs are online. Government agencies seek out public comments on their websites. Plus, activist groups maintain a steady stream of social media posts chronicling their various pet issues, who's involved, who's talking and what the likely outcomes may be.

Word travels fast. Everyone who cares to be can be—and will be—aware of what you're advocating for or against.

That has an effect on your member companies or individual members. Those companies are thinking about their customers and what their customers will think if—make that when—they hear of your positions. Things like: "If my trade association is lobbying against genetically modified food labeling, how will my customers feel about my brand and what it stands for?" Or, "If my trade association is lobbying against labor protections for workers, what does that imply about my company and its practices?"

That can lead to some thorny internal discussions about stances and actions. "It was easy to form consensus when you were doing work in relatively quiet circumstances," says Sean McBride, founder of DSM Strategic Communications. "Now, if I'm a food company and I've made a commitment to shareholders and consumers that I'm going to commit myself to full transparency around where it was made, ethically sourced ingredients, how can I be in the domain of a trade association taking a position that seems to be at odds with that?"

For associations, there's a counter effect to all of the scrutiny. When companies come under fire from public advocates or activists, their trade associations can quickly become their biggest allies. Suddenly, the same companies that wanted to own their relationship with their customers are turning to their trade association for help as an intermediary with media pressures or dialogue with government.

McBride points to the example of what's known as front-of-pack nutrition labeling: the idea that putting certain key nutrition facts front and center on packaged food will help consumers make healthier choices. A few years ago, pressure mounted on packaged food companies to increase the information revealed on those front-of-pack labels. The pressure wasn't just coming from government, though that was part of it. Media and health personalities like Dr. Oz started speaking out on the subject. The cause caught on. A well-known nutrition blogger with the nom de plume "The Food Babe" waged a fierce advocacy campaign. Then-first lady Michelle Obama got involved, too.

The industry, feeling under siege, needed help navigating. As pressure mounted, companies welcomed the voice and unifying force of the Grocery Manufacturers Association (GMA). Together with a consortium of food companies, the GMA worked with government to come up with a labeling program that would work for all parties—a program that didn't need to be federally mandated, a huge public relations win, because the industry promised rapid compliance. In 2014, the GMA and the Food Marketing Institute together launched a national marketing campaign around the initiative, called Facts Up Front. The program spoke straight to consumers with a huge advertising buy, including a five-minute segment with a dietitian on the Lifetime channel.[13]

Through its role in the discussions, the GMA had become a leading voice on the issue—a voice that was out in the public sphere. Not every member liked that the association was talking directly to the consumer, since that's a relationship the companies themselves were used to owning, McBride notes. But for the GMA, the move was a success, positioning it as a leader and a relevant voice.

While many associations aren't accustomed to wading into territory that may prove divisive for their membership, that's the risk relevant trade associations take in a more transparent world. "The impact of our instantaneous communications has forced trade associations to evolve. The ones who are well-positioned are the ones who get it," McBride says.

Part II
Relevan

ce

Are You Essential?

"We're worried about annual meeting attendance while the profession or industry that we work for is burning down." —*Scott Steen, executive director, the American Physiological Society*

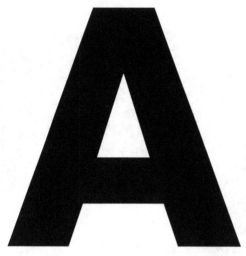ssociations have been around, in some form or another, for an amazingly long time. Colonial Americans were quick to form trade guilds, and the first official trade association in the U.S. predates the formation of the country: the Chamber of Commerce of the State of New York, which was formed in 1768 by 20 merchants.[14] It's still around today. A hundred years later, it was the Industrial Revolution and development of the late 19th century that led to the rise of dozens of trade groups, which banded together for both lobbying and business purposes.

Professional associations have a similarly long history. Some of the biggest, best-known associations have been around for well over a hundred years. The American Medical Association was founded in 1847.[15] The National Education Association began in 1857. The American Bar Association was founded in 1878.[16]

There were enough such organizations that in 1920, the American Trade Association Executives (now the American Society of Association Executives) came into being.[17] In the decades following, trade and professional associations exploded. Most of those organizations were founded to help companies deal with legislation that affected their business and sector. While publishing had always been central to scientific societies, it was the late 20th century—the '80s and '90s—when many of the trade groups started taking a broader view, serving as the center of trade shows and communications for their industries. Associations flourished and proliferated during that time—from 6,500 in 1958 to almost 23,000 in 1990.[18] Many of the associations followed the standard operational structure exemplified by big well-known associations like AARP, with a Washington headquarters and regional and local chapters.

That model lasted for about 30 years—the glory days, some would say—until a little more than a decade ago, when all of the forces I've already talked about really started to wreak havoc on the industry.

It started with the onslaught of disruptive technology and deepened as the Great Recession took hold. By this point, there were tens of thousands of trade and professional associations—92,000 in 2010, according to one accounting from the American Society for Association Executives—that had largely organized themselves around a model that was quickly becoming obsolete: centralized organizations making most of their money from member revenue and trade shows. When they were founded, and for all of their lives, if you wanted the knowledge, you had to join, and you had to be there.

Suddenly, you no longer had to be there. Not to learn, not to connect, not to thrive.

Much has been written and said about the demise of associations. There's a steady drumbeat of pundits predicting their decline—and has been for years. But you're still here. And you're likely to still be here in 10, 20, 40 years. I'm not here to jump on the associations-are-dying bandwagon. What I'm here to say is that I believe that if associations don't shift to a model where you're not just working on behalf of members, but adhering to a larger mission and proving it, every day, you may very well drift into oblivion.

Put another way, that core value proposition hasn't changed. But how you frame it and how you make it relevant to your members has. "Associations are still doing the same things we were 100 years ago—membership, meeting, publications—we're still making money that way," says Scott Steen, who was named executive director of the American Physiological Society (APS) in July 2018. "I can't think of any other industries that's true for."

Becoming Essential

What is "essential" changes with the times. Despite the tens of thousands of already-existing associations, the association market isn't necessarily saturated. There is still room for more as the economy changes: New associations pop up as new industries do, picking up the mantle of a young sector and becoming its voice. Take for example, TechNet, which calls itself "the voice of the innovation economy" and represents companies as diverse as Apple, PayPal and Airbnb.[19] The National Cannabis Industry Association was launched to contend with the many legislative and practical issues that come with the legalization of marijuana.

At the same time, other trade and professional associations drift away naturally as mergers and acquisitions chip away the dozens of companies that used to comprise a formerly flush sector. Some industries simply shrink or even disappear, taking their association with them. I'm thinking of pay phone manufacturers, for example. It's difficult to be relevant when a whole profession has ceased to be relevant.

Many of these professions have associations. But that doesn't mean that all associations representing dying industries need

> "Associations are still doing the same things we were 100 years ago—membership, meeting, publications—we're still making money that way. I can't think of any other industries that's true for."

The Robots Are Coming

According to a 2013 Oxford University study, out of around 700 occupations, 12 have a 99 percent chance of being automated in the future. Just eight have a 0.35 percent chance or less.

Which jobs are at risk?

insurance underwriters
mathematical technicians
sewers, hand
title examiners, abstractors and searchers
new accounts clerks
cargo and freight agents
telemarketers
photographic process workers and processing machine operators
data entry keyers watch repairers
tax preparers
library technicians

Which jobs are safe?

mental health and substance abuse social workers
recreational therapists
first-line supervisors of mechanics, installers and repairers
audiologists
emergency management directors   health care social workers
occupational therapists
orthotists and prosthetists

to fade into oblivion. It can be hard to see, when it feels like the walls are closing in, but sometimes there are alternatives if you begin to think differently about the future of the profession you represent. It comes back again to being comfortable thinking bigger, about your place in the world and the difficult changes that may need to happen to remain viable.

Take for example the Photo Marketing Association. Founded in 1924,[20] it was made up of mom and pop photo shops and the companies that take class photos for schools and other groups. A few years ago, according to someone who worked with the organization, the association was hemorrhaging money—careening from a healthy reserve fund to negative over the course of eight years. When the association had an opportunity to shift course and bring on board as members digital photo providers like Snapfish or online photo sites like Instagram, it recoiled. Leadership felt those new players were not on the same team—that they were undermining the market share of their members.

Fast-forward a few years, and the association eventually dissolved as an independent entity, becoming part of the Imaging Alliance.

Now imagine if the association had expanded—or shifted—its mission and welcomed Instagram instead of shunning it. Imagine if its perspective had been different. If instead of putting up walls and retreating to familiar territory, the organization's leadership thought about the best way to serve members and decided to help train them for a digital future. The outcome could have been very different.

In the thick of a struggle for survival, it's easy to put up walls around yourself rather than looking past them to see what's over the horizon.

But what about many of the rest of us—associations that represent growing professions but still face stagnant or shrinking membership? That's a question that weighed heavily on Steen's mind as he took the helm at APS in 2018. He inherited an organization with stagnant membership, one that was under pressure from associations that have built up around relevant, overlapping subspecialties. The organization had significant reserves, but the majority of revenue came from journal publishing.

There's no way, Steen says, to continue that trajectory. "If associations continue to think their mission is to produce meetings and journals and magazines ... they're not going to exist," he says. Instead, he says, it's time to recognize the pressures that face the industry the association represents—and *do* something about them. "We're worried about the annual meeting attendance while the profession or industry that we work for is burning down," he says.

So, what do associations do about it? Contrary to the way some have thought in the past, the future is not about ignoring or eliminating the meetings and journals and magazines. I'm not suggesting throwing the value proposition up in the air. It's about making what you do matter to members, to prospective members and to the broader world. You become relevant. More than relevant—you become essential.

You do that by determining not what you think your value is, Steen says, but by figuring out what that value means to your members. For APS, that means asking: What are the biggest issues in physiology now? The answer: The lack of funding for research and threats to the discipline as science and the way it's organized changes. These are questions that really matter, the big opportunities for associations to lead.

Those answers should inform the path forward for the organization. This part is important. If your profession's biggest issue is a lack of funding, that doesn't mean, Steen emphasizes, adding a panel at the annual meeting that talks about the lack of funding. It means thinking much, much bigger. Why not create a forum to bring together potential funders and those who need them to start creating actual solutions? Why not start a foundation to bring in money from funders? "Where's the big moon-launch effort?" Steen asks. "How do you solve members' actual problems rather than just talk about them?"

Moving in this direction—a major shift for most associations—means framing your thinking in a

"How do you solve members' actual problems rather than just talk about them?"

The wrong question:

How do we keep our
membership
from crashing?

The right question:

How do we create a thriving
membership that bands
together for a discipline
that moves toward the
greater good?

very different way. After all, I'm not talking about incremental change. It has the potential to be tectonic. It starts with the questions you ask from the very top of the organization.

The big question? What does the world need you to be? What *could* you be? That will give you a very different answer than if you ask how you boost membership or how to stop the bleeding. "Asking big, positive questions about what could be starts to move the organization in that direction," Steen says.

It may be a scarier answer, for sure. A riskier one, no doubt. But it's the answer that will propel your organization forward, rather than applying one Band-Aid after another.

Becoming Sticky

Once you've figured the path to becoming essential—those huge questions that will shape the future of the field—it's wise to also think about how to become "stickier." That is, how do you acquire that intangible quality that makes members think about you when they're not at your conference or consuming your content?

This isn't about membership and what makes people join associations—I'll talk about that later. This discussion sits at a higher level. It is about what makes people want to be around you, want to talk about you, want to be involved. It's what makes people think about your organization even when they're not physically present.

There are certain timeless characteristics that make people adhere to an organization, no matter what kind of organization it is, from an association to a summer camp to a vocational group. *New York Times* columnist David Brooks has explored this idea,[21] calling such organizations "thick." Thick organizations, he says, often have collective rituals or shared tasks. They also have a common ideal—or even better, a shared goal—and a distinctness in how they think, so they don't blend easily into other organizations.

This is especially important in a world where people are more focused on the individual and individual achievement and less adhered to organizations. "The current generation sees institutions as things they pass through on the way to individual success," Brooks writes. "Some institutions, like Congress and the political parties, have decayed to the point of uselessness, while others, like corporations, lose their generational consciousness and become obsessed with the short term."[22]

This idea directly links to my earlier point that associations simply must think bigger. By putting the organization in a much higher context—one that takes survival entirely out of the equation and asks how the association can have a bigger role in the world—you're naturally creating something sticky. You're creating an association where members have something important in common, something that fuels a sense of identity and belonging.

Becoming a "thick" organization

Thin organizations ...

Take advantage of people's strengths, treating them as resources to be used for various objectives

Have members who are there for mutual benefit

Thick organizations ...

Take advantage of people's desire to do good, triggering their innate longing to do and be more

Have members who are there to serve a collective, higher good

Reconsidering Your Purpose

"You don't buy Cheerios because you're obligated by Cheerios. I don't think the reality is any different in the association world." —Stephen Fox, vice president of membership and constituent relations, the American Nurses Association

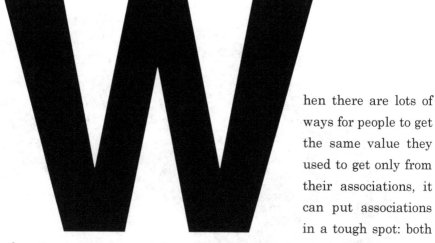

hen there are lots of ways for people to get the same value they used to get only from their associations, it can put associations in a tough spot: both when it comes to determining where the value lies and deciding how to deliver it. One way to start effectively thinking about value is to lift the conversation up a level—to your mission.

The Role of Mission

If your mission is clearly defined, it can help you determine how to best deliver it, how to determine what's truly valuable and what is secondary to that mission. Remember the Ohio Society of CPAs? Its mission is, in large part, to advance business in Ohio. Note how broad that is! When CEO Scott Wiley applies that mission to everything he's considering or thinking about, it becomes easier to see how to deliver value. It becomes easier to determine when to wade into political debates, as well as easier to determine which products and services to offer. That mission isn't just words on a page—it's a practical lens through which to view the organization's work and way forward.

The American Astronomical Society's Kevin Marvel uses a similar framework as a pressure test. It's a very different kind of organization, of course: The AAS's mission is "to enhance and share humanity's understanding of the universe." Everything the organization does—every action it takes—is built around that goal. That means building a series of events where astronomers want to come together to discuss the issues of the day. It means setting the bar for professional ethics as a means of supporting all astronomers. It means supporting young astronomers in various ways—including by making statements on current events—and publishing meaningful journal content.

One critical note: Being relentlessly mission-oriented, however, doesn't mean relentlessly poring over membership numbers at the expense of everything else. "Our mission is to enhance and share society's scientific understanding of our universe. It doesn't say with more members or to grow our membership base," says Marvel. "Having members is fantastic, but it's not the main way we achieve our mission."

No, You're Not Amazon Prime

I couldn't go much further without addressing the elephant in the room: membership. For many associations, the idea of membership has never been murkier.

On one hand, conventional wisdom says the whole association world is shrinking or stagnant. But that's an oversimplification. In fact, there's a bit of a bifurcation across the industry. Some, especially professional associations in fields that have seen fracturing due to a rise of subspecialties, or those with significant industry consolidation, are stagnant if not shedding members and revenue.

But others are, in fact, very much on the rise. For a few, that's a function of the times. There's a small but not insignificant subset of trade associations that are benefiting from a heated political environment.

Takeaway:
Use mission as a filter to apply to everything you consider, from when to wade into political debates to which products and services to offer.

A huge number of organizations experienced a surge of affiliation and so-called hate giving after Donald Trump's election. That's true not just for big-name nonprofits like the American Civil Liberties Union but also for smaller associations, especially in scientific fields, that have mobilized around hot-button issues. Take, for example, the National Infertility Association, which went to bat to allow women in the military to freeze eggs before going into combat and experienced a surge of support as a result.

For those in the former category—which applies to hundreds of associations that have been operating the same way for years, the inevitable question arises: Should you be chasing members? Is that the most efficient route to survival and revenue increases? It's fairly easy for someone like Marvel to sideline the scramble for membership: Dues are around 10 percent of the AAS's revenue stream. It's much harder to consider membership a secondary issue when it constitutes the bulk of your organization's income.

Before I talk about whether you should ramp up your race for members, let's talk about what membership is—and dispel another myth or two.

Some in the association space will argue that membership is very much in style—just look at Amazon Prime or Netflix and their membership models. It seems like everything's about membership these days, from dinner kits to diapers: everyone is trying to incorporate a membership revenue stream. There's a whole book on the subject, Robbie Kellman Baxter's *The Membership Economy*, which talks about the revolution in businesses using subscription formats to build a consistent lifetime revenue.

I'm not here to tell you that the membership economy doesn't exist. This new model—some might call it an entirely new way of thinking— can be truly a transformative one for just about

I take issue with the idea that we should all be somehow worshipping or emulating the Amazon model.

everyone who sells products and services. There's no question that more and more companies are adopting the model, hoping to take advantage of a world driven by subscriptions.

But that doesn't mean the membership economy can solve all of associations' ills. Associations aren't selling movie rentals or diapers or food kits, and I take issue with the idea that we should all be somehow worshipping or emulating the Amazon model. The key difference: Someone who is an Amazon Prime or Netflix member doesn't feel much kinship with other Prime or Netflix members. Their reason for joining is simple: monetary value.

If you try to operate like Prime, Dollar Shave Club or Plated, you may be shortchanging yourself. These retailers aren't clubs, or groups of people with any kind of meaningful commonality. This is membership with a small "m"—at an association, you want membership with a capital "M." You want members who appreciate the monetary value—but stick around for more than just that. They're there because they truly feel they're part of something.

Netflix, Amazon Prime and all the rest don't offer a model that associations can—or should—replicate. It's not that we shouldn't be looking to leaders like Amazon or Netflix for some tips on how to capitalize on consumer interest—nothing wrong with that. But to say that these are member organizations misses the earlier points I made about stickiness. The second that monetary value goes away, consumers won't hesitate to abandon Amazon Prime or Blue Apron. Associations have the potential to become much stickier—to have value that's not just monetary but much, much more.

The secret sauce is a mixture that combines relevant discounts and benefits and a feeling of belonging to something. It's something the most successful associations have mastered, from AAA to AARP to the National Rifle Association, which beyond its lobbying, offers access to local hunting clubs, shooting and safety classes; kids and family programs; gun insurance; free subscriptions to the NRA's magazines;

discounts at thousands of gun, sports and outfitter shops; and accidental death and dismemberment insurance.[23] Whether you love it or hate it, it's hard to deny NRA's success—and it's not just about politics. It's driven by a passionate member base and then sustained by a comprehensive suite of relevant products and services.

"For professional societies, the value of membership starts out transactional, for the discount, but after awhile they start to form a bond," says David Gammel, executive director of the Entomological Society of America. "That's the model—getting people to do things with you, even if just for the discount or being eligible for an award. Then they'll stick with you."

Knowing What Members Value

To thrive, an association has to have two parts of an equation: a clear and sustainable value proposition for members, and a stickiness factor. That's the formula for lasting success, the secret sauce, whether you obsess over membership numbers or not.

Marrying those two ideas is where the money is—the value creation that will endear members and prospective members to you, engendering stickiness and growth. That's the tack that Stephen Fox took when he stepped into the American Nurses Association (ANA) in 2011. He had spent most of his career in the private sector; ANA was his first association. The organization was built around membership, with more than two-thirds of its revenue coming from that side of the business. Membership was lagging, because of both the rise of outside opportunities for nurses to network and communicate, and because of the rise of nursing specialty associations that had the ability to be more relevant to certain subgroups in a time when more nurses were specializing.

The secret sauce is a mixture that combines relevant discounts and benefits and a feeling of belonging to something.

To thrive, an association has to have two parts of an equation:

a clear and sustainable value proposition for members

a stickiness factor

That's the formula for lasting success, the secret sauce, whether you obsess over membership numbers or not.

True to his background in marketing and brand, Fox knew that to grow, the organization needed to project much more relevance than it was—it had to start segmenting beyond one-size-fits-all. The challenge was how to maintain ANA's big tent—its appeal to several hundred thousand nurses across regions, ages and specialties.

To increase relevance, the association adopted a segmentation model. But how could it slice such a huge population? Fox knew that it could only handle a small number of segments before it would become too overwhelming. The staff talked about segmenting by role, education or job title—but if you focus on one job title over another, for example, you alienate huge swaths of people by giving the impression that one is less important than another.

The association also ruled out segmentation by specialty, since that was covered by other associations. It held focus groups and one-on-one sessions with nurses, probing into needs that cut across a critical mass of people. ANA found those needs in segmentation by career stage. As the conversations progressed, the researchers noticed that the concerns and needs were breaking out into three distinct groups: early career (first four years); up-and-comers (years five through 14); and nursing leaders, who have established themselves and are beginning to think about their legacy.

That differentiation allowed ANA to speak to huge numbers of members and prospective members—but still feel hyper-relevant for nurses at different stages of their careers. For example, the organization knew that for early-career nurses, bullying is a huge issue. It created a free webinar called "Surviving Bullying." Ten thousand people signed up in a week and a half. ANA used those signups to create a database.

The strategy is not comprehensive, Fox notes—"we haven't divided the world into three"—but those three groups represent the three biggest swaths of opportunity for the organization. Largely as a result of this strategy, membership was up 49 percent in the five years ending in 2017, Fox says.

No matter the type or size of organization, stickiness is about knowing who you are—and staying relentlessly true to that. The American Astronomical Society's Marvel recalls the fear years ago among associations as social media groups formed across professions. "Almost right away there was an astronomers Facebook group," he says. The group was started by six professional astronomers, with the goal of engaging other professional astronomers.

Initially, Marvel says, he and his colleagues were nervous—"It looked like competition for us." But it turned out that their nervousness was unfounded. "That Facebook channel isn't going to be a conference or a scholarly presentation. It isn't going to solve diversity and inclusion issues," he says. "It isn't taking away our value proposition." Instead, it became just another channel for communication, one in which the AAS occasionally participates.

Know Your Audience—and Your Potential Audience

For association leaders who are looking to boost membership, conference attendance, content consumption or purchases, the question of whether to allow student members often comes up. The American Astronomical Society grappled with that question back in the late 1990s, when the board debated and ultimately decided to allow students to present research posters at AAS meetings. The argument for allowing students to present, AAS's Marvel remembers, was that the organization should be nurturing the future of the profession. The argument against was the concern that doing so would dilute the excellent professional research.

At that first meeting with student posters, the group held its first ever undergrad reception, with 35 students and faculty advisers in attendance. Consider recent events: Seven hundred people attended 2017's student reception, with well over half of that number made up of undergrad students, Marvel says.

Expanding the tent to include students has had a couple of significant side effects, Marvel notes. One is that some of those students stick

Putting a Price on Membership

I would be remiss if I didn't tell the other half of the American Nurses Association (ANA)'s growth story. Segmentation and relevance were huge, yes. But it wasn't the only change that Stephen Fox's team made. They also lowered the price of membership. One of the things the staff heard repeatedly, Fox says, is that membership was simply too expensive: Members were paying an average of $300 per year. One of the organization's major pilot programs was to drop the price to $175, a 40 percent cut. That new price point, Fox says, has been a major growth driver. Quite simply, "it's easier to earn a value proposition at $175 than it is at $300." It's also easier to promote a $15 monthly payment—that's a palatable number for many people.

For ANA, pushing a lower-price strategy simply made sense, Fox says. That's largely because of the group's big tent. It knew there was a history of members and prospective members griping about the cost. Plus, less churn has meant more stability in revenue.

The reduced pricing model has grown revenue in every year in every state ANA has launched it. The pilot began in seven states, and as of 2018, has grown to 23.

For ANA, cutting prices makes sense. It has a huge base of potential members, with vast room to grow. Plus, many of its members have a second affiliation with specialty societies. For other associations, especially those with complex legacy structures that involve both state and national dues, simplification can make a big difference. For example, the Air Conditioning Contractors of America reported that new member sign-ups rose 60 percent after it launched a new, $39-a-month membership rate in 2015, which it advertised prominently. Members had been paying around $450 per year on average, so the new monthly rate didn't represent much of a change. But the new, simpler structure made a huge difference in an era when people simply aren't willing to navigate a byzantine structure. "We're an organization of small-business owners, so for a lot of our members it's more of a personal money decision than it is a corporate decision. You're talking about low sums of money, and someone's doing an impulse buy," Kevin W. Holland, senior vice president of business operations and membership, told *Associations Now*. "What we've found that works for us is someone comes to our site, and, if they're looking for something specific or they want to get a piece of information, it's very easy to get it now, at 39 bucks."[24]

around after graduation and become junior members: The fraction of junior members has gone up substantially. The other shift is that the community overall has become more accepting, encouraging even, of the fact that the association has the responsibility to nurture the next generation of researchers.

Other associations are similarly expanding their tent. The American Hotel and Lodging Association used to have a traditional model where members joined state-level affiliates and automatically became members of the national association. To expand membership and focus more on government relations, a few years ago the association allowed direct memberships to all segments of the hotel and lodging industry—a big expansion of the group's tent.[25]

When it comes to expansion of a potential member base, many of us remember that between 10 and 20 years ago, there was a tremendous push across associations to expand internationally. The thought was that it was a natural way to draw in more members, especially in stagnant fields.

Some associations have learned that the international strategy, while it makes sense for certain fields with gangbusters international growth, isn't for everyone. The AAS, for example, established an international affiliate membership class in the early 2000s with the intent of drawing in more members. The organization put a fair amount of effort in, including creating extensive communications in several languages.

One of the big advertised benefits was the ability to attend the annual conference, which takes place in the U.S., at a much cheaper rate. But many of the international members didn't want to or couldn't afford to take the trip. And there were even a few cases of existing members converting to a cheaper international membership just to get the conference discount. The international membership never really took off and eventually fizzled.

Another means of membership expansion comes from rethinking individual and company memberships. Today, especially in the face of industry consolidation, some associations are pushing toward a hybrid individual/company model.

In that case, a government agency or company may be able to purchase and grant "membership" to everyone in a department, giving all members access to information and publications. But not everything is included. This might be called something like a "professional staff" membership. Those department-wide members may get access to some content but not all, or some education but not the annual conference. In that way, these organizations are vastly increasing the community they're marketing to, with the potential for far more incremental revenue from webinars or conference attendance or other relevant content.

This strategy has become increasingly popular: Hybridization associations that combine company and individual memberships more than doubled between 2011 and 2015, according to Marketing General's 2015 *Membership Marketing Benchmarking Report.*

Even the American Society of Association Executives (ASAE) has moved in that direction. A few years ago, it announced that when an association joins ASAE, its staff is also included in membership. In the process, it dramatically raised the number of people it is marketing webinars and other paid content to.

Are Members the Ultimate Goal?

When growing membership is one goal—as opposed to *the* goal, you can be more flexible with your structure and experiment with different revenue models. That's what happened at the Entomological Society of America (ESA). "Membership is not the beginning and the end," Gammel says. "It's just one option."

That mindset opens the door to considering how nonmembers might want to engage with you—without converting. In essence, you're recruiting customers in addition to members—a new way of thinking about revenue for many associations. At ESA, for example, customers might attend an annual conference, paying a higher fee than a member does.

Go Global or Go Home? Deciding If Global Expansion Is Right for You

The Institute of Management Accountants (IMA) touted in a 2018 *Associations Now*[26] article that its membership has shifted from 90 percent U.S.-based to more than half non-U.S. Stories like these abound in the world of associations and lead many pressured association leaders to seriously consider flying their flag abroad.

It's not a decision to take lightly. While expanding internationally can help an organization bolster its membership and its clout, it also may come with land mines.

The move was a savvy one for IMA. China's business infrastructure is growing by leaps and bounds, and more and more businesses are setting up shop there. Those businesses need management accountants—the profession is growing in emerging economies.

The organization was careful before taking the leap, spending the time and money to incorporate Chinese language into its systems and its Certified Management Accountant exam. "You need to spend a lot of time understanding every facet of the local market," Jeff Thomson, CAE, IMA president and CEO, told *Associations Now*.

Global expansion can lead to thorny territory for associations that tend to issue points of view on political issues. Your international audience may be miffed if they feel that you're spending so much of their resources on lobbying for American concerns. It won't be long before they're saying, "Hey, what about us?" and demanding a voice on their own domestic or regional concerns.

Plus, you can't expect to treat international members the same way as U.S. members, especially if you're pushing into developing nations. You may need an alternate pricing structure. You may find that a key membership benefit like free or reduced-price annual conference attendance has little value, because some overseas members can't afford the required international travel. You could end up with unexpected consequences, like at the American Astronomical Society, where a few U.S. members converted to the cheaper international membership.

In short, global expansion isn't a panacea. When your discipline is truly global, expansion can make sense—especially if more of the funding growth is abroad than at home. That's the case for the American Geophysical Union (AGU) as the field of geology shifts toward Eastern economies, notes Executive Director and CEO Chris McEntee. Today, two-thirds of first authors in AGU's journals are non-U.S. based. The organization has ramped up the international presence on its committees, task forces and peer reviews. And it has kicked off a meeting partnership with Japan and is planning an inaugural meeting in China.

If your certifications are in demand globally, that's another indicator that a global footprint might be right for you. But going global, or expanding internationally, is not a blanket solution for a shrinking association.

Or, a customer might be a professor at an institution that doesn't pay for association dues—but that professor wants to publish with ESA. In that case, the professor can take advantage of an open access model, where nonmembers pay a higher fee to publish.

That hybrid approach—some call it a Chinese menu, where customers select an assortment of products or services that appeal to them—takes the pressure off membership and allows the organization to create value at different levels for different constituents. But it also demands a fundamental rethinking of how value is delivered. "I'm okay with that," says Gammel. "Now, membership is just one metric. Its relative importance has come down a bit." These days, Gammel says, ESA has around 7,000 full-fledged members and 3,000 "customers" who have some interaction with the organization, which might mean publishing, attending an event or speaking at a conference.

I know that for many associations, the idea of membership is never going to die. It's simply too baked into the association DNA. That's okay. But it's time to start thinking about it differently. Membership "is not going to be the cash cow that it was," says Erin Fuller, president of the association solutions group at MCI Group. When there are so many opportunities to "join" without paying, the very idea of membership has been cheapened. The problem, Fuller says, is that associations are stuck in their ways. "Even though we know the user experience has shifted, we're still measuring progress by head count."

Most associations feel as if they have to have members in part because even if dues aren't the main source of revenue, members become the market they sell to. Without members, there's no one to talk to about content that's for sale or events. In the traditional model, membership "drives revenue, but it also drives the ability to sell other stuff," Fuller says. It becomes a cycle that's nearly impossible to break.

What if you didn't need that captive audience to consume your content or to attend your annual conference? As Chris McEntee, executive director and CEO of the American Geophysical Union, says, "We're spending less time thinking about the researcher as member and are instead thinking about how do we serve the researcher whether they choose to be a member or not."

To do that, you have to come from a position of strength, where the never-ending crunch for membership revenue doesn't drive all of your decision-making. What if you could dramatically expand the tent of potential customers without having to spend seemingly endless resources trying to reduce member churn and recruit new members?

You can. I'm about to tell you how.

4

Talking to the Right Audience

"When new staff come on board I always ask them, 'What business do you think we're in?' Some talk about the industry; others say we're in association management. I say neither of those is true: We're in the marketing business."—*Peggy Winton, president and CEO, the Association for Intelligent Information Management*

nowing your purpose and being relentlessly relevant is the beginning of this new path. But it's not the end—or even the middle. Once you are certain what your purpose is and how to make that purpose relevant to your audience, your job now is to take a product people may not even know they want and make it essential. How do you do that? Marketing.

I'm not talking about the kind of marketing associations have done for decades, raising awareness among members, potential members and other key audiences, like lawmakers. That's all well and good, and you need to keep doing it. But I'm talking about spreading a message to the public, to the broader world. I'm talking about talking to people who have probably never heard of you and who probably won't ever become members.

Thinking Big—Even If You're Small

It may sound counterintuitive, but that outward marketing focus is more important today than it ever has been. Every company, even every individual, is relentlessly focused on its brand and message. Associations cannot be an exception. I won't mince words here: Marketing has the capacity to save you.

Forward-looking association CEOs realize this. In the more than a decade that he's been working with associations, Seth Kahan, who advises association leadership on innovation through his company Visionary Leadership, has seen more and more C-suite emphasis on a strategic path forward that's built around taking the value an association creates and communicating it more broadly. There are two steps to this. One is to think about how the field you represent can have a massive impact on the world. The next step is showcasing that impact—the value that comes from the profession of nursing or financial planning or geophysics.

You're showcasing that impact in two ways: first for an audience made up of your members, yes, as a way of inspiring them. You've probably always done that. But, maybe more importantly, you need to showcase this value publicly. That's where a new way of thinking about marketing strategy comes in.

You may think this doesn't apply to you, that your association is different—because you're a scientific society or business-to-business profession. You may think that your industry has no business broadcasting to the broader world. It would be a waste of resources. Not so. There's tremendous value from spreading a broad marketing message—one that will directly benefit not just your association, but your members. "Members always feel like the world doesn't appreciate them and doesn't understand what they do. Plus, how do you get universities to value physiology as a discipline and to fund it?" says Scott Steen, executive director of the American Physiological Society. Well, guess what? "Funders follow the public; politicians follow the public."

In some industries, you may find that members don't inherently understand that positioning. In others, they're well aware. Chris McEntee, executive director and CEO of the American Geophysical Union, notes

I won't mince words here: Marketing has the capacity to save you.

that in recent years, "there's a greater awareness on the part of the scientific community that they have relevance, but they haven't done an effective job communicating that relevance." That's where associations come in.

So then, it's time to start talking to the public. Executed strategically, marketing can change everything. The problem is that most associations weren't built with an emphasis on marketing. They were built to serve their members—steadfastly, diligently, but often quietly. That simply doesn't fly today. This is a very different way of thinking than just publishing a magazine that's distributed to members, or other communication that's focused on internal audiences. I'm talking about reaching for something bigger.

When you start to think about changing the external perception of your association, your outreach will naturally shift in both its focus and its content. Steen recalls his previous role as president and CEO of American Forests, a nonprofit that's dedicated to protecting and restoring forestland. When he took over, its best years seemed behind it. The organization had lost $3 million in funding during the nine months before Steen arrived. When he walked in the door, the way he viewed it, his mission was to reposition the organization for "another century of relevance." That meant by definition creating a very public profile.

One of his first changes, Steen recalls, was to update all of the public-facing parts of the organization, from the website to the staff overseeing communications. He made new hires, including bringing in a well-known expert on climate change. That expert soon led workshops in the 17 states that committed to upholding the standards of the Paris climate accord—a move that was well within American Forests' mission but guaranteed to resonate beyond the organization's typical audience.

It's critical to note that when it came to much of American Forests' outreach, the new intended audience wasn't just environmental science journals or niche publications where it had been featured historically or felt comfortable. The organization worked to get mentions in *The New York Times*, *The Washington Post*, even *People* magazine. That very public messaging, Steen says, immediately raised American Forests' profile and was instrumental in significant wins like getting much-needed grant funding.

The publicity had a kind of domino effect. Mentions in the media helped lead to grant funding. Grant funding helped lead to more good work and increased credibility to build high-impact programs and a broader public policy agenda. That new, scientifically driven agenda was built with specific communications planning around it, which led to more prominent media mentions. Those mentions helped fuel robust social media participation and even celebrity partnerships. American Forests in 2018 had more than 250,000 Facebook likes, up from 1,800 seven years prior. More importantly, membership soared, and the organization became much less reliant on the corporate support that had been its lifeblood and left it vulnerable to economic downturns and corporate budget cuts.

Infusing Your Operations

When you focus on marketing as a strategic priority, it changes the way just about everything is done for an association. I'm not just talking about the look and feel of your marketing materials. It should change the way you and your staff think, in and out of the marketing department. Everyone, in every position, should have a marketing orientation. "When new staff come on board I always ask them, 'What business do you think we're in?'" says Peggy Winton, president of the Association for Intelligent Information Management (AIIM). Invariably, the new staffer will respond with something about information technology or maybe association management. "I say neither of those are true," Winton says. "We're in the marketing business."

"Funders follow the public; politicians follow the public."

Winton has a background in technology marketing and, she says, she long ago realized that when it came to AIIM, the value of non-dues-paying members was higher than joiners who just pay their dues and don't engage. When people are interested in engaging—even if they're not a member—that leads to a community, a community that is constantly looking for products and services rather than consuming passively.

That realization changed how she thought about the business. The organization had already moved away from its big annual trade show, which was sold in the early 2000s to an expo management company. Instead, Winton says, her focus shifted to creating a broader community that could be monetized much more effectively. Her first job, she says, was to build from scratch a portfolio of content-driven programs. That year-round portfolio includes webinars, research reports and a variety of other content assets.

How much do users pay for those assets? In many cases, nothing. In fact, "80 percent of what we do is free," Winton says. She's not concerned about giving so much away because of the model she's built. One of the association's challenges, Winton says, came as its audience shifted in recent years.

Information management has always struggled to feel like a true "profession," because its practitioners stretch across so many disciplines—it's truly horizontal. That reality became even more pronounced as the profession grew from specialists to those who were doing that job but within a particular line of business, like health care or manufacturing. In many of those companies, tech decisions aren't being made by technology specialists but rather by the line of business. Those people simply aren't interested in becoming members in an IT association year after year—but that doesn't mean they don't have needs that AIIM can fulfill on a one-off or short-term basis.

> When you focus on marketing as a strategic priority, it changes the way just about everything is done for an association.

On the flip side, AIIM serves sellers of technology—so the organization serves both the buy side and the sell side. So, the association created a model that's mutually beneficial to its buy-side and sell-side audiences. On the buy side, a membership is still available—$169 per year as of 2018. That allows access to certain premium content, virtual events and access to ongoing help with challenges, as well as training and certification—and is most relevant to career technology professionals.

The sell-side audience has become a larger part of AIIM's business model. Those companies love the line of business consumer—the one who's less likely to become a lifetime member—Winton says, because they are usually shopping for a technology solution for the first time. They are often actively seeking solutions because they've been tasked with a particular technology challenge. "There's value in the extended community," Winton says. "Not only in customer potential with our vendors, but infinite value in the intelligence they provide."

Those sell-side vendors have become key partners in the production of content. They might pay $15,000, for example, to be the exclusive sponsor of a webinar, or they might underwrite research on a particular topic and get featured in the resulting research report. There are two key elements that make this model work. One is that they become part of the educational offering. The other is that the content remains educational, not sales driven. AIIM often creates a content piece for the vendor, for example, positioning the vendor within it.

Winton's marketing background means she knows all too well the importance of measurement. Because so much of the organization's strategy is built around content that's free to consume, AIIM is relentlessly

> When it came to AIIM, the value of non-dues-paying members was higher than joiners who just pay their dues and don't engage.

focused on data collection. The community, as Winton calls it, is made up of 150,000 active subscribers—that is, those who have raised their hand and agreed to take some kind of qualified action, like downloading a white paper, that enables the organization to know who they are. From there, the focus is intensely on nurturing and tracking leads—all through marketing automation software HubSpot. Using those leads, AIIM staff can see how well content is performing, which topics are resonating and who's most engaged. The whole operation, Winton says, revolves around the intelligence the organization is constantly collecting and responding to. "That's the point where most associations fail," Winton says. "They don't consider themselves the marketing machines they should be."

A New Face to the World

One of the great democratizations of the internet era has been the idea that even a small company can look big. A startup founder can sit in her basement or garage and present just about the same professional, polished website that a Fortune 500 company can. She just needs to take advantage of the right technology and present the right face to the world.

Association leadership can learn a lot from that model. Many association leaders view their marketing through the lens of what used to be: a newsletter that's emailed to members, a high-profile speaker that draws members to the annual conference.

Sometimes the most effective marketing strategies come from thinking not necessarily about changing the value proposition, but reframing how you present that value to your constituents and to the world. That's the scenario Larry Gottlieb faced a few years ago running the Hudson Valley Economic Development Corp. (HVEDC), a small organization whose mission is to promote business in the Hudson Valley region of New York, north of New York City. (He later moved to a role at Nicholas & Lence Communications in New York City.) The organization, which was founded in the early 2000s, used what Gottlieb calls "a classic Field of Dreams model: If you build it, they will come." After the recession

Takeaway:
Whether you like it or not, you are in the marketing business.

struck, that logic was dead in the water. Nobody was coming. Instead, the organization shifted its mindset and began looking at who was already thriving in the area and needed help taking things to the next level.

It's the same mission it had always had, the same value proposition—to help businesses grow and thrive in the area—but a complete rethinking of how that value proposition comes to life, based on the bigger picture of relevance and audience need.

Gottlieb started by considering industries with potential: what types of area businesses were trending in the right direction and had the potential to grow with a little help. He thought of those groups as "clusters."

The first cluster HVEDC focused on was food and beverage. Those businesses needed connections and advice, so that's what the organization focused on. The initiative got a name: The Hudson Valley Food & Beverage Alliance. HVEDC commenced a series of educational talks called Nibbles. The region's first Beer, Wine, Spirits & Cider Summit was held in 2013. All of the initiatives had the goal of connecting entrepreneurs with similar problems to solve. It's not all that different from what the organization was founded to do—it just does a better job of identifying potential members who have the same needs and bringing them together to form a community, something that's important and hard to find for many small business owners. "You basically are branding something that already exists," Gottlieb says.

Communicating that you understand and can help is tremendously appealing when you're speaking to someone who suddenly feels that you "get" them. That's what happened, Gottlieb says, when HVEDC decided to form a cluster around life sciences and biotech. The organization reached out to area life science companies and invited them to a meeting on the campus of a local medical school. Out of 84 companies, between 50 and 60 showed up. "No one had ever reached out to them before," Gottlieb says.

"You basically are branding something that already exists."

Gottlieb listened as the leaders of those companies said there were three things they really wanted help with. One was for the Hudson Valley to be recognized as a valid geographical area for the industry, a true hub for life sciences, so they'd have a larger voice to garner state support for growth. Second, they wanted networking opportunities. And third, they wanted to market the region as a hub for life sciences to help with recruitment. Those were all things that HVEDC was able to do— thus fulfilling the organization's mission and at the same time, raising its profile. The clusters, in turn, become "artificial centers of gravity"— magnets for other businesses that want to reap their benefits.

Part of the reason the shift in strategy has been effective, Gottlieb says, is that it's reflective of the way the world works today—and doesn't try to operate on an outmoded model the way many associations do. For one thing, the strategy is in touch with the needs of its constituents: growing businesses. It doesn't assume that you can treat a craft beer brewer the same way you treat a life sciences or 3D printing company. HVEDC is "down in the weeds," Gottlieb says. "That entrepreneur, they want to talk to somebody who understands their marketplace. They don't want a brochure and for me to say that for a hundred bucks I'll give you access to some services."

That part is key. It's what makes the organization sticky and competitive in a world where up-and-coming entrepreneurs are already connecting on LinkedIn and a thousand other digital venues. HVEDC isn't trying to compete with those outlets. Instead, it's focused on its own, highly specific value proposition and how it gets communicated. It's the same value proposition, brought to life in an entirely new way that acknowledges the unique advantages of the organization. At HVEDC, "I'm creating a network within a community," Gottlieb says. It's local, it's rich, it's real life, not virtual. As the reach of events and content expands, when a new business owner begins to research funding, staff or locations, "If an entrepreneur connects into that community, at some point you're going to connect to me."

Branding Certifications

Let's talk for a moment about associations that focus on certifications. If you're in the business of providing certifications and continuing education, your focus is likely on increasing the supply of certified professionals in your field. You want to certify as many people as possible, especially if there are other places your members and prospective members could turn for continuing education. But what if you could actually increase not just the supply, but the demand for certified professionals? What if you could help make certification something that your members' customers and clients are seeking out—thereby dramatically increasing the need for certified professionals?

You probably can. Again, it comes back to marketing. When Kevin Keller joined the Certified Financial Planner Board of Standards as CEO in 2007, the organization already had a strong growth curve of financial planners ramping up to take the rigorous CFP exam, which allows them to advertise as a certified financial planner. Within a year of coming on board, Keller began a series of town hall meetings with members to see how they could be better served. What he heard, over and over again, is that while members valued certification immensely, they wished that more people knew about it. Not people inside the industry, but potential clients. People who probably didn't know much about financial planning and weren't reading trade pubs or the financial press. They wanted the public to be aware that those letters after their name translated into financial planning advice that's a cut above the competition.

The organization launched a series of quantifying research that corroborated what Keller was hearing: Spreading the word about CFP certification could dramatically increase demand for planners who had passed the test.

The problem: How to pay for a campaign to spread the word? Keller went back to the members and asked a pointed question: Would you be willing to pay more to maintain your certification if the extra funds were earmarked for a public awareness campaign?

The answer: a resounding yes. CFP Board raised fees from $180 a year to $325—nearly double. The organization has spent $75 million so far promoting the certification, completely funded by the additional income from fees. Meanwhile, the member retention rate actually edged higher—to 97 percent, from 96 percent, a rate that has held steady. "The strategy is very simple," Keller says, "and that is to make certified financial planner certification the must-have designation for those providing AND those seeking financial advice."

The outreach has included ad campaigns and press junkets—entirely new territory for the association. In the last five years, CFP Board has launched a corporate relations department and called on top brokerage firms like Merrill Lynch and JP Morgan to promote the certification among their legions of financial advisers. "Everything that we do focuses on does this advance either the supply or the demand for certified financial planners," Keller says. According to CFP Board, the total number of advisers holding the CFP designation has risen 43 percent since 2007.[27] It's incredible evidence of what's possible when an organization identifies its value proposition and communicates it broadly and effectively.

The Mythical Millennial

"There are differences in generations. We sat with grad students and professors as they used online resources. It was quite revealing." —Robert Harington, associate executive director, publishing, the American Mathematical Society

et's get it out of the way. You need millennials. The generation born between 1980 and 1998 now makes up a larger chunk of the workforce than any other generation: There are more of them working than Gen Xers or boomers. Even though many of these workers are now well into their 30s, we're still treating them like a workplace novelty: Thousands of articles have been written about how to engage this generation, a cohort that happens to be in many cases drifting away from association membership.

The proposed solutions generally fall into a few categories: Make membership free, make content more engaging, and make everything digital.

There's been so much frenzy about this audience, but much of it is surface level. Pundits throw around a lot of so-called solutions to connect with this audience. The reality is, it's not enough to make things cheaper, or digital, or add a bunch of shiny graphics to the materials you produce. To understand how to speak to young professionals, you first have to separate fact from fiction and distill trends from material, meaningful shifts in how people communicate and seek out information.

What's really different about millennials? Let's break down the breathless articles and fear-mongering speeches and figure out what sets this generation apart and how that really applies to associations. I'll start by taking some commonly held assumptions about this generation and considering whether they're actually true.

Myth No. 1: **Millennials are immune to marketing.** Reality: Nonsense.

Millennials have brand favorites just like the generations before them do. Just because they're not the same brands 50- or 60-year-olds love doesn't mean those preferences don't exist.

We're talking about a generation that is practically obsessive about anything showcasing the Apple brand. And what about coffee? Advice to eschew Starbucks is a tired trope constantly trotted out to cash-strapped millennials, because they're so addicted to it. Then there's Procter & Gamble brand Always, which has endeared itself to young women with its "Like a girl" ad campaign and now scores consistently high in surveys of millennials' favorite brands.[28] No matter how you measure it, the brand preferences are there.

I might even argue that millennials like marketing. If nothing else, it's second nature to them. This, after all, is the first generation where people have become brands, the generation that came of age with the Kardashians. Every young person with a Twitter feed or Instagram account is, in effect, branding and marketing themselves, and they realize that, curating their content to tell a certain story and carefully selecting their photos to convey a certain image. Unlike those who are older, for millennials who came of age selling themselves to the world through a social media profile, marketing is natural to them—it's part of who they are.

The conclusion here is that they're used to and completely comfortable being marketed to—but not the way their parents are. It's no longer all about splashy TV campaigns and catchy slogans. Younger people live in social media and are constantly responding to messaging there. I'm not talking about banner ads. I'm talking about affiliate links on influencer sites or participation in social sites.

The Takeaway: Marketing isn't bad. Far from it. If anything, the pervasive marketing of old has become like wallpaper: something that's just there, that young people tend not to pay attention to. To really break through, you need to speak the right way, at the right time, in the right place. You need to talk with them, not at them. That means engaging in two-way conversations and helping solve problems—the way the most effective brands do via social media. This is a key insight, one that I'll return to later.

Myth No. 2: Millennials won't pay for anything.
Reality: They're selective.

This is the generation that pays for streaming online content, rather than cable, for example. They pay for music services but don't buy full albums. They download apps but don't buy newspapers.

Paid content is certainly not dead. Not even close. But the value equation has changed. If you've spent your life buying just the one song you love, rather than an album, or streaming a single show rather than a full suite of cable channels, you start to think everything should be customized—and customizable—to your needs and interests. And you might begin to think that content or programming or a membership with a wide net damn well better deliver value if you're going to be willing to pay for it.

But there's more to this story. The other critical reality to note here is the incredible load of student debt and the finances of younger people overall. Many of those under 40 have it tougher than Americans of similar ages in decades past. Across a variety of financial metrics, this is the first generation whose finances are lagging those of their parents:[29] Young people have more debt and lower income than their parents did at the same point in their lives.

Plus, the well-documented explosion of student debt colors how young people save and spend, with good reason—imagine if you were making $40,000 a year and spending $800 a month on student loan payments. It would probably change what you considered essential and what you considered discretionary. "One of the first things I had to deal with when I came [to ANA] was the idea that membership was sold by obligation—it's your obligation to support your association," says the American Nurses Association's Stephen Fox. "That argument goes nowhere with millennials. They don't feel any obligation to pay money for anything."

The Takeaway: It's about value, value and value. This generation will not join an association out of a vague sense of obligation. Value must be clear—and it must be clearly communicated.

Myth No. 3: Millennials are more altruistic than previous generations.
Reality: They care—but so do the generations before them.

This idea is trotted out with every new generation that enters the work-force. Every generation is going to change the world, focus on altruism,

Whether or not millennials are uniquely idealistic is irrelevant.

eschew big corporate interests. Remember the hippies, a half-century ago? Hippies were all about tolerance and the rejection of materialism. Sound familiar? And then those boomers turned into 1980s, *Dynasty*-watching yuppies. That's all the lesson we need that glomming onto broad generational truisms is a recipe for disaster.

The fact is that young people, as a group, tend to be more idealistic than older ones. This has always been true, for a variety of reasons, and is likely to always be true. But whether or not millennials are uniquely idealistic is irrelevant. The fact is, younger people will always care about certain causes and generally be more cause-oriented than older ones. Knowing that should change how you talk to them and about what, regardless of some kind of blanket generational label that's being tossed around in the media. Understanding the difference in mindset between youth and experience will apply not only as you talk to millennials today, but also as you talk to the up-and-coming members of Generation Z, who will soon leave America's college campuses and join the working world.

I'm not advising you to ignore notions of making the world a better place. Quite the contrary. I want you to communicate that mission-first orientation to millennials and to keep it up as the next generation starts to join the workforce in the next few years. Keep in mind, too, that as millennials get older and progress in their careers, they're going to have increasingly pragmatic concerns. Their focus will be on promotions and management and work-life balance and all of the same things that prior generations were concerned about.

The Takeaway: Mission is important—but certainly not at the expense of value. The key here is that being mission oriented isn't enough. This drives straight back to the idea of being essential. To be essential to younger people, you have to show your place in the world—and show how your organization is the exemplar of your profession's role in making the world a better place.

Myth No. 4: **Millennials have no attention span.** Reality: Yes, this one is pretty true.

One study from comScore showed that online ads targeted toward millennials have to be around five to six seconds long to be effective[30]—which doesn't say much for the traditional and expensive 30-second TV commercial. But they're not the only ones suffering from the syndrome of the shrinking attention span. Technology has changed all of us. We all read less long-form content and are accustomed to information delivered via short bursts, whether that's an alert on our phone or a tweet. Not to mention, it's been years since smartphones became ubiquitous: The image of a 20-something staring at a phone screen has long ago given way to pretty much everyone staring at a phone screen, all the time. In the last decade, consumers across the age spectrum have begun to consume content on their phone, which necessitates and gets people used to shorter content that's easier to consume on the go.

Plus, the lack of concentrated attention is really about more than just depleted attention span. The

> Our goal is to break through the messaging about millennials—some of which is useful, some of which is bunk—and talk about the lasting changes in the way people interact with organizations and consume information.

abundance of choice in media and content overall has a direct effect on attention. This is why some people constantly change the channel on their TV, hoping to find something better. People in their 50s grew up with three choices of TV channels. People in their 20s grew up with 300.

The idea of boundless choice extends beyond media. Some people would say the problem with sustained attention is also due to the havoc that dating by app has wrought—millions of people, overwhelmed by choice, constantly looking to trade up.

The bottom line: Everyone has choices these technology-fueled days, probably too many. The combination of a constant barrage of content and the abundance of choice for consumers means you don't have a lot of opportunities to get your message across. To be effective, your messaging needs to be clear, focused and easy to distill.

The Takeaway: Consider that young people both demand more value for the dollars they spend and have a shorter attention span than ever. Take those together and you can forget members for life. You have to prove your value over and over again—and you have to prove it quickly.

What This Means for You

One thing I want to be very clear on: I'm not advocating jumping into trends for the sake of trends or turning your back on white papers because "20-somethings hate to read." Yes, we've all heard this one. Don't worry: Your future is not solely dependent on Snapchat. Our goal is to break through the messaging about millennials—some of which is useful, some of which is bunk—and talk about the lasting changes in the way people interact with organizations and consume information.

Many of the technology consumption and usage shifts that started with millennials simply because they were early adopters of technology now describe how pretty much all of us behave. That means that what we expect from the companies and organizations we interact with has changed in just a few short years. For examples, chances are, you consume much more information on your phone than you did just five years ago. You may have changed how you subscribe to media and content. You likely do a lot more communicating through social media than you did just a few short years ago.

This isn't about obsessing about millennials and trying to appeal to them at the expense of older members. This is about acknowledging that millennials—and the Generation Z workers coming up behind them—are at the leading edge of many shifts in how associations communicate and act when it comes to association and membership. Evolving to accommodate what are becoming widespread, fundamental changes is essential to the future of your organization, no matter who your target market is.

5 Steps to a Millennial-Friendly Association

The good news is that many of the strategies I've been talking about—being pointedly mission-based, deemphasizing traditional membership—are inherently appealing to the younger generation. The key is not just to cultivate a value proposition that's grounded in those ideas, but also to communicate it in a way that resonates with a tech-savvy, always-on, mission-driven population.

In true millennial style—the listicle—here are five steps to make your organization focused on millennials and future generations, without falling prey to passing trends.

1. Be Digital First—But Not Digital Only

When it comes to millennials, the channel you share that content on is especially important. You have to be where they are: Millennials expect information to be convenient—and, unfortunately for you, the meaning of *convenient* varies from person to person. One thing is consistent, however, for those accustomed to using a phone or tablet for just about everything: Convenient almost always means digital. The American Mathematical Society's Robert Harington notes that when the AMS sat down with both grad students and professors to study how the two groups interacted with digital content, the differences were stark: Younger researchers were more facile with online discovery and comfortable ingesting information digitally. More senior professors were moving in that direction but still relied heavily on print.

If you're tempted by the idea of going all digital, though, my view is that it's usually a mistake. Some associations feel pressured to go 100 percent digital to stay current and try to simply drop their existing information into this space. The result? Uninspiring flipbooks that merely reprint magazine content, a barrage of self-serving Facebook messages, a multitude of uninspiring blog posts or email newsletters full of clichéd stock images. When it comes to messaging, associations that throw themselves headlong into a digital-only approach can end up alienating both younger members who crave authenticity and older ones who are accustomed to print. "Math is contemplative," Harington says. "Print and electronic will coexist."

Without a doubt, there's still power in paper—maybe more than ever. Tony Rossell, senior vice president of Marketing General, notes that the impact can be material: He sees much higher renewal rates with paper-based memberships. "I still think that paper makes a difference," he says. I agree. Imagination's research shows that a print magazine is routinely among the top three benefits that association members most value.

I'll talk about this more in the last section of the book, but the precise content distribution mix varies from association to association, depending on who your audience is and what they need. For some industries, print can be a critical differentiator, as it is for the National Business Aviation Association. "Publications are great for the brand," says Chris Strong, senior vice president of conventions and membership. That's partially because older members expect them. But it's also a reflection of the fact that in an era where so many print publications have faded away or gone digital, a tangible publication carries even more weight.

No matter what, you need to cover a healthy mix of media with your specific niche or industry in mind. Experiment with upping your frequency and sharing information via social media (for example, Facebook Live broadcasts), print (magazines, newsletters, books), video (YouTube tutorials, videos embedded in your email newsletter) and audio (podcasts).

2. Don't Forget to be Human

A bone-dry content style will not endear you to millennials, who are leery of corporate-speak in all its forms and have come of age with the much more casual speak of social media as their tone-setter. Loosen up the tone of your communications, but don't go overboard and risk alienating members by suddenly ricocheting from a style reminiscent of a corporate news release to emoji-laden, acronym-riddled content (srsly!). Not to mention, millennials can see right through your inauthentic attempts at mimicking their style. [eye roll emoji]

Part of being human, too, goes back to not just the words you use, but your behavior—especially in social spaces. Young professionals have been communicating in social media virtually their entire lives. They expect conversations, not one-way communication streams where content is being pushed at them by a faceless entity. You have to be there. You need to respond and be a part of the conversation.

When you talk, be prepared to listen—and talk back. Have a staff member monitor social media and other platforms where you offer content, and respond to anyone who comments. Using Google Analytics or similar tools to analyze where your website traffic is coming from will help your staff focus on the platforms your members use most, and free social media monitoring tools will allow them to stay on top of social media mentions so they can quickly respond.

3. Put the Mission First

Remember the story about the American Astronomical Society speaking out about Black Lives Matter? That idea—that it's the association's job to support its constituents even in areas outside the organization's traditional realm—was first floated by a millennial member. Of course it was! Younger members are attracted to the idea that the association has a larger mission. Take advantage of that. Think about ways your organization can support your younger members as people living in the broader world—not just with tactical professional tools.

When you put the mission first, you're in the best position to compete with the online groups and other organizations vying for people's attention. The AAS's Kevin Marvel recalls that several years ago, six astronomers started an astronomers' Facebook group, with vetted membership, designed to attract professional astronomers. While that looked at first like competition, "it ended up being another channel for us," Marvel says. That's because a Facebook group is never going to be able to position itself as a leader advancing a mission—setting the bar for professional ethics and advancing the profession. "It's not taking away our value proposition," Marvel says.

It comes back to your relevance. This is where you can shine among your younger members. They want to have a sense of purpose—and you are in a position to give that to them, much more so than many other sources of information.

So be loud and proud about your mission. Put it first. Incorporate it in your content, your events, your communications.

4. Embrace the On-Demand Model

On-demand isn't just about millennials—but because younger people have grown up this way, it comes up most often when talking about those under 40. All people—but especially young people—are accustomed to getting things when they want them, how they want them. This is a generation that has grown up watching TV shows on demand—no planning their schedules around their favorite shows. The shows essentially plan around them. Same for shopping, which is at their fingertips 24 hours a day. Spotify brings perfectly curated music instantly, everywhere. Instacart. Uber. The list goes on. When it comes to consumption, gratification is immediate.

For associations, that means rethinking how you structure membership. The days of one-size-fits-all are probably behind you. The AAS's Marvel, for example, says he knows that paying for ongoing membership is going to be a hard sell for many young people just coming out of school. That's why those people can access professional development without becoming members. The way he sees it, that model is true to the mission; after all, "enhancing our understanding of the universe means always having a pipeline of students who have the right skill set."

I'll talk more about specific membership models in the next chapter. But however you structure it, a monthly newsletter and annual conference won't be enough to engage this generation. Whether it's knowledge content, certification or networking, prepare to be always on and always available.

5. Provide Human Interaction

I've been talking pretty much this entire book about the importance of being digital. I'm not going to back down from that. But the human touch is still important—in-person interaction isn't going away. But it's changing. "The individual has so much more power than in the past. You used to have to rely on your society to [market yourself] for you," says Harington of the AMS. But that doesn't mean there's no role for community—it's just that the role has changed.

Today, it's less about shaking hands and making connections—you can do that, to some extent, digitally. It's about connection. True, meaningful connection. This is good news—it's not so different from what associations have been doing for decades. "The idea of learning from people who do the same things you do, that's still at the core of what people get from an association, and it's hard to get from other places," says Scott Steen. "The ability to be recognized by your peers is still tremendously important and hasn't been filled in other ways."

But how associations deliver that value has to change—and change fast. Again, it comes back to relevance and mission. You have to have a relentless focus on what younger people need from those human interactions. That may mean building communities around topics or issues that are particularly important to early careerists. Or maybe it means offering networking sessions for younger members who are inclined toward job hopping. You still have to offer connections—but they must be contextualized and hyper-relevant.

Taking the Next Step

If you're considering making millennial-focused changes to your strategy, don't just feel around in the dark: Ask them! Survey your younger members to find out exactly what they want and then give it to them. You could ask, for example, what types of content they find helpful, who they'd most like to network with and what kinds of events they'd like to attend.

But, beware the potential land mines with this tactic. This generation wants to be part of the conversation, not a target market. Instead of sending a cold survey, where you and your members are constrained by a set of questions, go out and have conversations with members in real life. Talk to them at your events. Invite especially active young members for a chat over coffee. If you have volunteer committees, ask for one-on-one time to chat instead of just relying on group feedback.

Questions arise naturally when you're talking with a member in real time. As the questions go deeper and deeper, you'll find the answers you're looking for—and they may not be what you were expecting.

The Association of the Future

"I keep this clipping on my desk: 'People only get upset with organizations that matter.'" —Kevin Keller, CEO, CFP Board

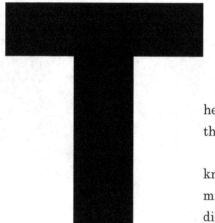he million-dollar question: What does the association of the future look like?

Answering that question starts by knowing your value proposition. It may not look all that different than it did a few years ago. But it may need to evolve, get bigger, even, in the face of the opportunity to position yourself as a leader in an industry. Consider the American Nursing Association. Stephen Fox notes that information and networking is still a critical part of the value that ANA delivers. But the availability of that information is huge and constantly changing.

Your value proposition is critical—but it's not the end game. Now you have to deliver that value. This is why members come to you in the first place—and how you're going to attract future members. People and businesses should join your organization because you offer something of value that they can't get anywhere else.

The Association of the Future ...

... Has a story to tell

You can do a bang-up job of delivering information and knowledge. You can have a truly effective certification program. You can host a must-attend annual conference that brings together the who's who of your industry.

Today—and tomorrow—none of that is enough. For your association not just to survive, but to thrive—to become the sticky organization that people return to over and over again as an essential part of their lives— you need a story. That story should demonstrate how your value fits into the context of a rapidly changing world. That's something that differentiates you from the countless sources of information and so-called thought leadership that your members have to choose from.

In that way, you give your members what they crave in an increasingly complex world: a tribe, something to be a part of.

Here's how Ed Liebow, executive director of the American Anthropological Association, frames his organization's story. First, he says, he considers just about everything as a part of the association's story to tell: affordable health care, a mysteriously disappearing Malaysian airliner, even pornography. It's all fair game. "There's almost nothing you can read in the headlines today that hasn't been studied by an anthropologist," he says.

Next, the association sifts through current events and the urgent news going on in the world and determines what to build a policy agenda around. This way of thinking—with urgency, with an eye toward anthropology's role in the broader world—"has in effect set an agenda not just for the association but for our members, by giving them a more focused way to direct their passions and intellectual firepower," Liebow says. "That's why we go into this line of work, to use the tools we have to help society."

And that's not all. By doing that, by setting an agenda and being a part of the conversation, "we look like leaders," Liebow notes.

That perspective isn't limited to trade associations. In fact, it's urgent, it's imperative, that professional associations become part of something larger, too, in order to stay relevant. The most relevant associations, the ones that are building a framework that not only protects them from the winds of change but makes them essential, are figuring out how their organization can be at the forefront of a movement within a sector or industry.

Thinking that way naturally engenders engagement. Entomological Society of America Executive Director David Gammel says ESA has made a concerted effort in recent years to "look at the biggest picture and place entomology in that context." That effort is twofold. Part of the effort is to focus on entomology as a career and make sure the organization is at the forefront of issues like diversity, inclusion and harassment. The other half of the effort comes from looking at the world's big issues, the truly global problems where entomology can be relevant—and making sure that relevance muscles into the organization's agenda. Then the association becomes part of the broader societal conversation. In ESA's case, leadership narrowed it down to sustainable agriculture, public health and climate change—three huge areas where the public might not always think of the science of insects, but where entomology can play a huge role.

That's what Gammel was thinking about when mosquito-borne disease Zika broke out in Brazil in 2016. ESA quickly reframed an already-planned event to be more urgent, to talk about the disease and its impact. Because of that event and its timeliness, ESA was invited to a summit convened by President Barack Obama in D.C. That was a huge win, because the conversation around epidemics like Zika is typically led by the medical community, whose perspective during epidemics like Zika is something along the lines of, "We'll also have an entomologist who will kill all the bugs," Gammel adds wryly. By purposefully framing the entomology profession and its association much more broadly than that—as an organization that can help with sweeping public health goals—ESA was elevated in the minds of policymakers and the public. For associations, this kind of success comes down to one big idea, Gammel says: "You have to look at mega-trends and how they relate to you."

Consider American Forests. When Scott Steen took the helm, the organization was focused on getting grant money to facilitate planting trees in forests. A noble goal, sure. But not one that felt particularly relevant in a 21st-century world with endlessly complex and nuanced environmental needs. In a shift, Steen took a forward-thinking, science-based approach—including hiring scientists. The organization learned to identify which forest ecosystems would have the greatest long-term environmental impact. Then it built coalitions with other organizations and worked toward a science-based, on-the-ground restoration of forestlands. At the same time, the organization made sure to build out communications plans to tell the story to both the public and policymakers, getting the organization broad recognition. "The approach is much more comprehensive and sophisticated," Steen says. And much more compelling for members to get behind.

To start thinking this way, Steen advises, ask yourself: What does the world need you to be? Think, for example, about an association representing a discipline with math or science. What a time to be sitting in that seat—just as STEM initiatives have become of paramount importance. If you're that association, your mission may not sound that different than it always has—probably something about promoting the profession and furthering research.

But don't stop there. How that idea fits into the world has changed immensely. A math or science association has the opportunity to think much more broadly, to promote the *idea* of math and science, to think about and solve for

"You have to look at mega-trends and how they relate to you."

contemporary issues of diversity and education. When you frame the question as what the world needs you to be, it will help you think in that bigger, bolder direction. It will help you begin to build your story.

The Association of the Future ...
... Champions its audience

So you have a mission. How do your members embody that mission? How do they demonstrate the incredible work the profession does in the context of broad societal challenges?

Chances are, you know some of these answers already. You probably feature members in your magazine or invite them to speak at your conference. But are you telling the stories in effective ways? Probably not.

Steen, who runs workshops on storytelling, gives the example of the American Ceramic Society, which represents ceramic and glass engineers and scientists. You know the type: "Their presentations were chemical equations in 12-point Times Roman on PowerPoint slides," Steen says. But behind the dense façade lay remarkable, human stories. There was the glass scientist who figured out how to encase nuclear waste in giant glass spheres that could be buried deep in the ground. There was the scientist who used his friend's liver cancer diagnosis as motivation to invent a more effective cancer treatment that uses microspheres of glass to isolate radiation to tumors within the liver.

"That's the story of ceramic science," Steen says. "That's why it's important."

The story of how your members exemplify your mission can help you in a number of ways. It gives credibility and a human face to your mission—like the incredibly powerful story of the scientist who invented a new cancer treatment after a friend's diagnosis. The stories also elevate your members in their profession—something an association is uniquely positioned to do.

Promote your members' stories. "That's a critical part of what associations need to do," says Steen, "tell member stories in powerful ways." That's because, whether or not your members realize it at the time, when you help put their work and their stories in the context of the big problems your profession is helping to solve, you're doing more than shining up their image. To frame their work differently—bigger—may help them be more competitive for funding or get more visibility for their department.

You can start small. For example, the International Interior Design Association has different segments of its membership, including students, take over the association's Instagram account throughout the year. That means IIDA's younger members get a chance to show their stuff, and IIDA's Instagram feed benefits from a fresh perspective.

The American Geophysical Union takes member involvement a step further. For the last couple of years, the organization has tapped its members for help with everything from renovating its headquarters to infusing technology into its meetings. The organization issued an open API challenge asking members to submit a plan for a new way of collecting and disseminating data at its big fall meeting. The mission was broad, encompassing serendipitous discovery of relevant research, discovery of new collaboration opportunities and identification of emerging areas of science. The first-place winner collected $15,000.

Not all queries for help come with a potential cash prize. Members are helping AGU come up with plans to monitor information about energy and water use in the organization's newly renovated headquarters. They're helping to determine how the data is collected—for instance, at the level of the workstation, the floor, the whole building, etc.—and how the data is displayed. In turn AGU will make the data available to the community for anyone who wants it for their own scientific research. Members, says AGU Executive Director and CEO Chris McEntee, are eager to help. "We've never had anyone say no," she says. Including the organization's data-savvy members helps them "view us as not so distant from them, of greater relevance." Plus, she adds, it helps add an element of "street cred" to the plans and changes AGU is making.

Including your members may not be something they're asking for. But it's certainly something they'll appreciate. Beyond that, the more your members are involved, the more your association keeps its pulse on the latest developments in the industry, keeping you top of mind. "We're trying to increase more direct relevance by embracing and involving the scientific community in what AGU does," McEntee says.

The Association of the Future ...

... Talks to everyone, not just its members

This next part is critical. Once you have a story, it's time to tell it. And not just to your members, though that's a start.

This can be especially valuable for an association that issues certifications. It's all well and good, after all, for your members to feel proud of their professional credentials. But if those members' clients and customers don't demand the certification, it's not worth much.

That's why the value of certification became the key element in CFP Board's story. CFP, Kevin Keller notes, has both a mission and an obligation to work for the public's good—to make sure financial planning is done competently and in the best interest of the clients being served. Investment advisers can dole out financial advice; so can brokers. But Certified Financial Planners have passed a rigorous exam and are licensed and regulated. In an industry where people are handing over the keys to their life savings, and financial institutions face deep skepticism, trust is enormously important. Making the public aware of the rigorous

What makes a story worth reading?
Key elements:

standards that come with CFP certification isn't just in the best interest of CFP Board—it's key to the organization's mission. "Awareness,"
Keller says, "is a strategic priority."

That push for awareness translated into several initiatives. A public awareness campaign included advertising across social media, print,
radio, even TV's CNN and NBC Sports. The idea: Most consumers
wouldn't dare visit a doctor or hire an exterminator who isn't certified, so
why do it with a financial planner who doesn't have the Certified Financial Planner certification?[31] "In many ways, we're creating a profession,"
Keller says. He envisions a time, he says, when financial planners are
regulated, like accountants or attorneys.

Until that happens, developing and overseeing a licensed profession
brings with it some thorny moments. When you toughen and vow to
enforce standards, that inevitably means some of your members aren't
going to meet them. And just like a rogue attorney can make a state's bar
association look bad, or an incompetent physician can make a medical specialty board look bad, a certified financial planner who's not acting in a
client's best interest can raise negative publicity in a way that it wouldn't
if the organization weren't continually pushing into the public eye.

Keller views public airing of grievances about planners who have
allegedly violated standards as something that comes with the territory
for a licensed profession. "It gives us credibility," he says, even if it sometimes brings an unwanted spotlight. For him, that has translated to a role
that's more in the public eye than he anticipated when he took the job.

A public-facing focus can dramatically change how your organization is perceived—that's true for just about every profession and type of
organization. And whether you're putting an ad on during prime time,
publishing an op-ed or getting mentions on NPR, the goal isn't always just
to spread the word to the broader public. Steen knew that when American
Forests pushed to get mentions in the mainstream, popular press. "A lot
of times the real value wasn't the public," Steen says. "We used public
engagement to leverage very specific moves." In American Forests' case,

that meant a strategy to earn grant money, which flowed as the organization became more public and its reputation soared.

The Association of the Future ...
... Evolves its membership model

When your members and prospective members view membership as transactional, rather than a lifetime commitment, you have to position it very differently. A few years ago, International Society on Thrombosis and Haemostasis (ISTH) Executive Director Tom Reiser says he was determined to get associations to stop looking at membership as "such a sacred cow."

Recalibrating doesn't mean doing away with the membership altogether. But it does mean reconsidering the model that may have worked in decades past but is no longer relevant in a world with rampant competition for time, money and attention. Today, many forward-looking associations are doing just that—rethinking their membership model to reflect a way of thinking that's much more transactional. "Membership still matters a lot," Reiser says. "But now it's less about how much we can cram into a membership from a product and services standpoint—it's more about what is important to you." That point of view also inherently fosters community, a critical point for any association that wants to become sticky.

One way to approach the new world of membership is simply to think differently about the value you're providing—to laser focus on delivering relevance. That's the tack that the American Nurses Association took. The organization's career stage segmentation model—with different content and benefits for early career, midstage and later career nurses—has made the association appear much more relevant to its target market, which is 4 million strong. Dovetailing with that change was that membership price cut to $175, from $300. Though the reality is that many members had effectively paid around $175 in the past because of discounting, the new, consistent pricing is more stable and has contributed to lower churn, Fox says. Membership at ANA is up 49 percent in five years, from a combination of the new pricing and the increased value that comes from much more tailored offerings.

Price cuts aren't right for everyone. A greater departure from tradition can be found at organizations that minimize the importance of membership, deriving revenue from other sources and walking away from the member-counting, member-chasing game. At the American Astronomical Society, membership isn't the only path to accessing benefits. Nonmembers can still access professional development. They can still access tools like meeting support, which provides logistical support for those planning meetings or conferences. All of these nonmember activities, Kevin Marvel notes, generate revenue—and when you do that, chasing membership becomes less imperative. "I could drop membership by 30 bucks, and my membership would go up by a factor of two. That doesn't mean I'm doing well," Marvel says.

For a few, a new model may mean eschewing traditional membership altogether. AIIM President Peggy Winton notes that several years ago, she discovered that the monetary value of the non-dues-paying members was much higher than those who just joined, paid dues, and didn't engage in any other way. It was then that she decided to focus the organization's energy on building a broader community that could be monetized—but wouldn't be considered "members" in the traditional sense.

The idea was to become less reliant on a traditional membership model with a single, annual trade show. Instead, the association pumps out hundreds of pieces of content on an ongoing basis—a year-round portfolio of programs including webinars, research and editorial assets. "We knew that the broader community that we could build through content assets would be monetizable and would give us lots of opportunities and rich intelligence as well," Winton says.

AIIM still has a membership option—the organization calls it a premium subscription—that costs $169 a year and allows exclusive access to certain content and discounts on training and certification. For others who aren't interested in that level of engagement, they're able to access a huge well of free content and pick and choose what they want to pay for, whether it's the $1,100 annual conference or a $49 short online training course. That approach also benefits the organization because it gives access to the huge population of people who aren't necessarily information management professionals but have a one-time need. That population wouldn't have been interested in joining an information management association on an ongoing basis, but they may be willing to pay for a webinar or course that addresses a specific, timely need they have. Part of the objective is to create content that courts this larger community that's larger than AIIM's traditional member base—making programs and products that are more consumable for them, Winton says.

Those people, who aren't members but select individual content or educational elements that suit them, are considered subscribers. Today, there are 150,000 active subscribers in AIIM's community—meaning they have all raised their hands in some way or another, agreeing to download something or taking another action that qualifies them and gives AIIM access to a trove of data.

Overall, Winton notes, the organization's revenues haven't changed much, but staff is way down and the margins are much, much better. Today, AIIM derives 65 percent of its revenues from the subscription side of the business.

Making a membership transformation takes more than a shift in strategy and tactics. It's a full-blown mindset shift, one that can be uncomfortable. But if you're doing it right, losing members doesn't mean the

"I could drop membership by 30 bucks, and my membership would go up by a factor of two. That doesn't mean I'm doing well."

value is eroding in the organization. It just means that the balance has shifted. "Membership is just one option," says Gammel. "Someone can do a lot of stuff with us and never be a member. Fine—you're a customer. I'm okay with that."

The Association of the Future ...

... Supports inclusivity

I can't talk about relevance—and becoming essential—without talking about inclusivity. For many professions, growing outside of a historically white and male base has never been more urgent in an era of reckoning over the treatment of women and minorities across the United States and beyond. In the current climate, if your role as an association is to elevate a profession, prodding that profession to a more inclusive future is a manifestation of your mission. A more inclusive profession is one that's in step with a changing world.

Take financial planning. One of the challenges of the financial planning industry, says Keller, is its "overwhelmingly male and Caucasian workforce." Moving beyond that—promoting the role of women and minorities—isn't lip service for CFP Board. It makes the CFP certification more relevant and more valuable to those who have it, Keller says. A more diverse profession leverages the value of the organization for an urgent, larger social problem—making it relevant and essential. "We're looking to do not what others are doing," Keller says, "but what's out there that needs to be done."

In 2016, CFP launched a Center for Financial Planning with the objective of creating a more diverse and sustainable financial planner

> "Someone can do a lot of stuff with us and never be a member. Fine—you're a customer. I'm okay with that."

workforce—creating a pipeline of diverse talent. The Center has a broad suite of initiatives, including offering scholarships to those who want to attain CFP certification, conducting research and doing outreach to young women who might want to pursue financial planning as a profession. The "I am a CFP Pro" campaign promotes financial planning careers with a hashtag and personal stories from young financial planners.

The program is particularly appealing to big financial firms that employ financial planners and have historically faced the world with an overwhelmingly white, male face. To date, the initiative has raised more than $10 million in donations and sponsorships, including millions from big financial firms that historically have had trouble filling their ranks with women and people of color.

For many associations, inclusivity is simply one strategy to advance the mission of elevating the status of the profession they represent. That's what the Ohio Society of CPAs decided when it evaluated the idea of launching a three-year diversity and inclusion program. OSCPA's membership is becoming more socially conscious as it skews younger, there's no question. But urging from younger members wasn't Scott Wiley's main concern—especially in a state with sharp-edged political divisions. "LGBT is not a social issue for us," Wiley says. "It's a workplace issue for us. Why would we want to do anything to prevent talent from wanting to work in our state and think it's a good place to be?"

And so OSCPA's diversity inclusion program was born. The program includes research and conversations with top state businesses to figure out how diversity and inclusion can be part of a strategy to make Ohio a draw for businesses and workers.

"We're threading a needle very carefully," Wiley says. "But we'll do whatever it takes to make business grow in Ohio. Then Ohio's going to have the workforce it needs, create good jobs and create opportunities for CPAs."

That attitude is part of a transformation that touches every part of the organization, Wiley says. By homing in on things like diversity and inclusion—issues that are mission critical, even if they're controversial—"we are trying to transform our organization to what creates and delivers value."

The Association of the Future ...

... Rethinks education

Your organization probably has a few ways it's been delivering education for years. An annual conference with tracks of content, webinars for continuing education, daylong seminars for credentialing. Whatever it is, most organizations have made only tweaks to their strategies since the advent of web-based learning more than a decade ago.

Now's the time to revisit how you're delivering education.

In Ohio, CPAs need 120 hours of continuing education every three years to maintain an active license, and a minimum of 20 hours each year. For years, OSCPA had delivered a comprehensive, thorough suite of education options: 35 to 40 conferences each year and 150 half- or full-day seminars. Plus, the organization offered on-demand web-based courses that might be an hour or two long. Leadership started thinking about the explosion of YouTube learning: people watching short videos to learn how to repair their air conditioner or pave their driveway. They looked outside the profession, delving into conversations on the future of learning. The idea of nanolearning was born: mini-lessons, as short as 10 minutes, that could be delivered whenever a CPA has a few minutes to spare.

Ten minutes may sound crazy. But Wiley realized that not all continuing education is created equal. Some topics demand a daylong seminar, no doubt. But something like a single update on an accounting rule could easily be delivered in 10 minutes, giving members exactly what they needed in a uniquely accessible way.

The problem: Ohio's accreditation board didn't approve learning in increments shorter than an hour. OSCPA had to lobby the board, proving that it was possible to deliver real, meaningful education in just 10 minutes, which it did by showing that it could measure the learning. Once the board agreed with that, it took the better part of nine months to write, edit and rewrite the legislation allowing for the microlearning.

As of 2018, the microlearning program was more than two years old, with 40 10-minute courses that are available on demand. A 10-minute course might cost as little as $5, compared with $29 to $49 for an hour-long course. Even with those price points, it's one of the more profitable products in the association's online portfolio, Wiley says. That's partly because the organization can be incredibly efficient when making the courses, taking a 30-minute live program, for example, and dividing it into multiple shorts.

For the OSCPA, the benefits are more than financial. Ohio was the first state to offer nanolearning for CPAs—13 states did as of the end of 2017. It also stands out as a point of innovation for young members and prospective members. "It's a great business opportunity," Wiley says. "It also demonstrates thought leadership for us as an association."

Nanolearning may not be right for you. But the idea is to consider how the consumption of information has changed—and how that applies to the content and education you produce. It may mean delivering content on Facebook Live or streaming talks the way TED does. It could mean adding virtual reality technology or bringing in experts to moderate live web chats.

The point is to move forward.

For many scientific societies, rethinking education means reconsidering the journal publishing model. For the American Mathematical Society, that meant thinking more broadly about what it was publishing and who the audience was. The association recently purchased a 10-year licensing deal with the Mathematical Association of America,[32] allowing the AMS to dramatically increase the number of books it's producing. While MAA's books are lower level, with an audience of educators rather than researchers, Robert Harington isn't concerned. If anything, he says, access to a wider audience makes a traditional academic society more relevant. Plus, expanding the association's body of work jibes with a profession that's sending its practitioners more and more out of traditional academic centers, into actuarial work, hedge funds and finance companies.

For any journal or publication program, tracking key performance indicators is critical. Data points like article downloads and author satisfaction can help you determine if your program is structured the right way.

The Association of the Future ...

... Evolves events

Events have long been the bedrock of most associations' value proposition, and I'm certainly not on the trade-shows-are-dead train. "The big conference with a lot of people doesn't seem to be going away," says the AAS's Marvel. "Despite all the ways to meet, there doesn't seem to be a lot of desire to not get together in person."

But that doesn't mean you can get away with running your conference or trade show the way you always have. In many industries, for-profit conferences have encroached on what was traditionally associations' domain. And in others, budget crunches or consolidation have meant much lower attendance.

Plus—and this is maybe the most important part—when there are so many things competing for your members' attention and time, whether it's a competing event or just the sense that they don't need you because of an active professional social media circle—your events cannot feel the same as they did 20 or even 10 years ago. Everything about delivering information has changed: technology, attention spans, budgets. Your events must change, too.

In short, your event has to feel like an experience. Booths in a trade show hall and tracks of speakers are no longer enough. After all, it's easy to channel the typical speaker experience through a webinar. Chris Strong, senior vice president of conventions and membership at the National Business Aviation Association (NBAA), wants to make sure that when members leave the annual trade show, they feel as if they've been through a common experience. The conference now includes a display of more than 100 aircraft. Recent speakers have included Sully Sullenberger, the pilot who famously landed a damaged US Airways airliner in the Hudson River in 2009, and astronauts and brothers Scott and Mark Kelly. The investment for the event has just about doubled, Strong says, part of a "change in philosophy" that the organization is fully committed to.

But updating the event isn't enough. How do you know if your changes are resonating? Strong says he's increasingly focused on key performance indicator data that's tailored for trade shows. While much of the technology is in its infancy, it has the potential to revolutionize what we know about conferences and events. Things like heat mapping can show how many people are going into an area at a given time. Tracking technology can help show sponsors how much more traffic they get to a certain location on the trade show floor or where to place a banner if they want the most eyeballs. "All of a sudden I can use data to improve ROI," Strong says.

Putting so many eggs in the trade show basket isn't for everyone—but it's something that works for many, despite the hysteria a few years ago about the death of the trade show. For some industries, yes, trade shows may be on the wane. But for others, they remain mission critical. Part of a strategic plan should be to evaluate which activities generate the most revenue and therefore are most critical to update. If running a trade show constitutes $10 million out of a $15 million budget, then it probably deserves a lot of energy.

At ASIS, the global association for security practitioners, the trade show comprises 55 percent of net revenue—but CEO Peter O'Neil was wary of being put in the box of being considered just a trade show producer. "I gutted my marketing," he says.

Instead of a trade show, the annual event morphed into a "learning lab," with mini education sessions and product demonstrations. That updated language alone helped prod people to the show floor. In addition, the organization made sure there were high-profile attractions on the show floor that attendees couldn't get anywhere else, like a theater, swathed in a black curtain—making the floor a destination in its own right, not just a collection of booths. "We're trying to demonstrate to our members that there are different ways to learn," O'Neil says.

This evolution holds true for scientific societies too. The American Geophysical Union has made a concerted effort to contemporize its meetings, considering the ways people consume information. Posters can be interactive rather than static. The digital boards allow scientists to use a touchscreen to access figures, tables and data sets that fuel the results being presented, for a more robust presentation.

AGU is also rethinking how meeting floors are structured. Rather than organizing in alphabetical order by scientific discipline, the poster area is being broken out into "neighborhoods" that bring certain, interrelated research areas together. It's all about "helping [attendees] find the content and the people they want to interact with," says AGU's McEntee.

The Association of the Future ...

... Doubles down on content that matters

Way back in 1993, *The New Yorker* published a cartoon that featured a dog sitting at a computer and telling his canine friend, "On the internet, nobody knows you're a dog." Today, that dog is probably writing best-selling books and running a community of 500,000 members— because on the internet, nobody knows whether you're an expert or not. Everyone and their mother-in-law is sharing their insights to boost their authority. The problem? This phenomenon is chipping away at the perceived value of your association's content.

Content—once the bedrock of an association—remains at the heart of associations' future. But not just any content. As a content provider, you have several advantages over the dozens of talking heads and self-proclaimed experts shooting off provocative tweets and publishing white papers full of platitudes. The first step is to take a hard look at the content that's out there and determine what you can do better. Chances are, that's a lot.

When the American Nurses Association launched segmented content designed for nurses at different career stages, it resonated because the organization had tapped into a strategic direction that maximized relevance. When a free webinar called "Surviving Bullying" garnered 10,000 signups in a week and a half, that was because the content was incredibly powerful, and it came from a source that nurses intrinsically trusted—their association. Creating important, resonant content didn't just galvanize existing members, it also "attracted nonmembers to our orbit," says ANA's Fox.

Proprietary content that's service oriented and can't be created by other organizations remains hugely important to associations, a way of demonstrating their unparalleled access and intimate knowledge of a profession. No one else, says NBAA's Strong, has the authority to issue a compensation survey that shows what companies are paying business pilots or airline mechanics. NBAA is able to charge a premium for niche content like that. These days, he says, "We're much more aware of what people are willing to pay for."

The same goes for the Metals Service Center Institute, the association representing metal producers. For years, the organization provided free access to valuable, proprietary research content. That widespread access eventually eroded the content's value. For-profit companies are freely "borrowing" the information for their own data sets, says Chris Marti, chief information officer and vice president of data analytics and

Journal Publishing in a New Era

The calculus is a bit different for academic associations, many of which were built around classic journal-publishing models. Many of those organizations have found that partnerships and other arrangements that expand their reach are hugely beneficial. Take the Entomological Society of America. The traditional subscription model was "under duress," as David Gammel puts it: Big publishers were encroaching, and at the same time, scientists had different perspectives on how they wanted to share their research. In 2015, ESA began a partnership with Oxford University Press. It in effect established a true open access journal, where scientists pay a fee and their articles are freely available to the world—to more than 3,600 institutions, including 1,400 sites in developing nations that receive free or deeply discounted access.[33] That means that ESA's name, and its members' content, is reaching a vastly different market than it was before.

AGU, too, has launched four new open-access journals in the last few years. A few years ago, the association moved from a self-publishing model to a partnership with publisher Wiley, allowing for broader reach and marketing as well as technological updates. In addition to the new open-access journals, today AGU has been able to add enhanced commentary and a preprint server where researchers can post their meeting posters and research results in advance of a conference. While the change wasn't easy—there were plenty of naysayers who thought the association was shedding its responsibility to the scientific community—today, submissions are up and so is content production. Plus, AGU is better able to reach critical global markets it couldn't before.

executive education. The association recently began the process of clos-ing access to that content for all nonmembers, to protect the investment and the intellectual property, as well as rebuild the cachet of the studies and data. For so long, Marti says, associations didn't have to compete in this way. "You were in a proprietary space and didn't have to do it." No longer, particularly as for-profit companies encroach on the space. "We're not going to let you publish our stuff and analyze our stuff, often not very well. This is proprietary stuff that they can't create on their own."

Plus, in light of research that showed that members were hungry for marketplace data and forecasts, new reports are also being introduced: specific, niche reports about metals end-market activity like automotive or light trucks. Those will be individual market reports, published quar-terly and available as an annual $1,000 subscription. It's all part of a strategy to intensify production of one-of-a-kind, deeply intelligent, rel-evant content—the kind that differentiates the association and creates value for members.

Not all differentiating content is printed. Consider Goldman Sachs. Yes, that Goldman Sachs. The white-shoe investment bank holds peri-odic live events called "Talks at GS," where the mission is to "convene leading thinkers to share insights and ideas shaping the world." Notice that there's nothing in that mission about finance or markets—the heart of Goldman's business. The programs are intimate, one-on-one inter-views with high-profile thinkers across an incredible range of fields and disciplines. Recent speakers have included actor Edward Norton, balle-rina Misty Copeland, Cardinal Timothy Dolan and soccer superstar and philanthropist David Beckham.

What do those speakers have in common? Virtually nothing, on paper. But with each new interviewee, each new high-profile speaker who agrees to sit in front of the Goldman Sachs logo, the firm gains clout, its brand is modernized, and it accesses tens of thousands of people who otherwise aren't familiar with the company. Early on in the initiative, Goldman posted the sessions—which can be as much as a couple of

Google =
stuff

You =
careful
curation

hours—on YouTube, and they recently expanded to Hulu, Amazon Prime and Spotify.[34]

It is a brilliant content marketing strategy in the age of TED talks, one that humanizes a company that's seen as disconnected from mainstream America, all the while cementing its role as one of the most influential firms in the world. What does it have to do with you? A lot. Just ask Larry Gottlieb of the Hudson Valley Economic Development Corp. HVEDC is not a huge organization, or one with national scope. Gottlieb realized a few years ago that in a digitally driven world, "that one-on-one discussion is becoming more vital." That was one of the realizations that led him to create intimate networking events for like-minded area businesses.

But he didn't stop there. He recruited Foursquare founder Dennis Crowley to headline a local event talking about disruptive forces to business, like the gig economy, and how to best adjust to them.[35] "People said why would an economic development organization do that?" Gottlieb remembers. "And why shouldn't we do it?"

Gottlieb likens the approach to Facebook inviting the Dalai Lama "to talk to a bunch of coders." It's about leveraging credibility—and using others to build it. After all, not all influencers are found online.

The Association of the Future ...

... Curates, curates, curates

Talk to forward-thinking association executives and consultants and the idea of curation comes up over and over again. After all, creating high-impact content can be a labor-intensive undertaking. It's less so if you're not creating all of it yourself.

I know what you're about to say. Curation has become something of a dirty word in some circles, a reminder of the old internet content farms that practiced unscrupulous "borrowing" from other sources in order to build their own content databases. And to be clear, I am not talking about morphing into one of the many "thought leaders" who simply curate information or post opinionated summaries of the news. You'll also notice that many of the thought-leader posts on social media are engineered to generate likes and clicks. There's a mass of generic take-aways such as, "Work-life balance is important" or "Success is what you make of it." These pithy posts may garner thousands of likes, but are they truly serving your members better than you can?

Industry knowledge is *what you do*. For associations, curation can be an incredibly powerful tool. While there's a lot of knowledge out there, "a lot of it is crap," says Liebow of the American Anthropological Association. "One of the things we do really well and people will recognize the value of is to be the curator of high-quality knowledge. Some will be satisfied with Wikipedia, but that won't serve their long-term interest."

> Industry knowledge is *what you do*. For associations, curation can be an incredibly powerful tool. While there's a lot of knowledge out there, a lot of it is crap.

So how do you position yourself? One way to do it is to become the hub, the center of gravity that vets information and makes the call on whether it's worth your audiences' time. "It's about how you curate and surface: What's the intelligence you can glean and then put back out there?" asks AIIM's Winton. "You are the hub. You have to start thinking about it that way."

There are a lot of ways to do this. Consider highly regarded publications like *The New York Times*, *Wired* and Quartz that publish carefully considered roundups of the week's news. In doing this, they are serving a very specific value and promise: They are telling you what you should read. They are, in essence, editors telling you what's worth your time, giving you a content diet in a world of infobesity. In order for a reader to value that service, the organization providing it has to have a certain clout. And as associations, you do. Your members trust you to distill what matters. Take advantage of that trust—use it to provide a service. Be the marketing machine that associations have a right—and a duty—to be.

In this way, you're not trying to compete with the scientists. You're not trying to compete with the self-proclaimed thought leaders publishing on LinkedIn and tweeting with abandon. Your role is to police what's out there and apply a layer of judgment to it—and make sure your members are getting the best content all the time. A roundup or newsletter or magazine that is made up partly of proprietary content and partly of existing content is incredibly valuable as a branding exercise: It shows the layers of value your organization provides. Plus, it establishes you as the leader you should be, with the authority to create the right editorial cocktail across your profession.

The side benefit to operating this way is that when you take on this exercise, you will quickly discover the white space: the useful content that could be produced, that isn't out there and freely available for your members and larger community. That's your cue to step in and create that content.

You know how busy you are? So are your members. Use the power of your brand equity to become a distiller of information and the arbiter of what matters.

The Association of the Future ...

... Puts data front and center

None of what I've outlined so far—the membership strategy, the events, the content—matters a lick if you're not using data to make decisions.

Data should infuse everything from deciding how to structure your events to determining what time you post social media updates.

Many associations have made baby steps here. You might use Facebook's reporting tools. Rely on Google Analytics to see which search terms you're ranking for. But I'm talking about something much, much deeper—and much more comprehensive.

Start at the beginning: with basics. Ask your members what they want. "If you don't ask your members and your constituents—people you could bring into the organization—and listen to what they say, how do you know that you're doing the right thing?" asks the ISTH's Reiser. At the ISTH, the education needs assessment the organization undertook—one of the first steps in a broader strategic planning process—was critical, Reiser says. It helped determine what needs the association's members have day in and day out, so it can tailor its offerings accordingly. Sure, Reiser says, the organization knows its members and probably would have gotten close if it had forgone the full analysis—but close isn't good enough anymore. "Given the expertise of our board and committees, we probably wouldn't be 180 degrees off track. But a few degrees can make a huge difference."

But don't stop there. After that "environmental scan," as Reiser terms it, consider the differences between your different groups of members, so you're not applying one-size-fits-all solutions. Marketing General's Tony Rossell recalls that with one association client he worked with, 80 percent of sales were coming from 20 percent of members—but the association was treating everyone the same.

Data and analytics can end that practice, helping you make the most of your marketing. Why are you trying to sell a $10,000 product to a recent college grad? Why are you pitching a webinar to someone who regularly attends deeper, in-person sessions? Slicing the data you may already have access to can help you create a series of personas or segments to differentiate components of your membership—much the way that the American Nurses Association did with its content around career stages.

That will help you get the right message in front of the right person at the right time. "People can talk all they want about differentiating, but most have no idea," Rossell says. "Maybe 90 percent of associations have no idea of the age of anyone in their database. There's a big disconnect between that theory and the practice."

If that describes you, start smaller and incremental. Look for opportunities to incorporate basic benchmarking tactics like A/B testing and return on investment analysis. Analyze which membership signup tactics garnered the bigger response: a discounted rate or an introductory offer. The beauty of data analysis is that it allows you to tweak as you go, making small changes that may have big impact. Test and learn is the mantra.

When you work that way, "It's easy to try things in an iterative way without betting the farm," says ESA's Gammel. ESA, for example, looked at how many scientists were presenting a paper at an event. It turned out that 90 percent were presenting, something that many scientists have to do to secure new funds. So rather than advertise for the conference in order to grow attendance, the organization issued a call for papers. That outreach, though, was highly tailored: ESA knew which subdiscipline the scientist was working in and what meetings he or she had attended in the past, and tailored the marketing accordingly. The organization was able to add between 10 and 20 percent to attendance that way.

This approach works particularly well when you can think about the information you have in your database and apply it in really tailored ways. For example, ESA's marketing team might figure out who lives within driving distance of a meeting and reach out more heavily and with specific messaging.

When AIIM evolved its strategy to build out a broad community, Winton says, she knew that broader community would offer more than just a group to sell to—that it would offer endless opportunities for what she terms "rich intelligence." People were coming back to the site because of free but highly educational programming, and harvesting intelligence could go a long way toward reducing the expense of outbound email and other advertising. Because the content marketing program is run through marketing software provider HubSpot, she is able to see what information is resonating with different groups, who's consuming what and which formats are most successful. "We started nurturing leads and tracking leads," Winton says. "Behavior trumps profile any day."

The data enables more customization: When you know what people want and need, you can create for that need. AIIM, for example, has been able to create learning paths for people who reach out with specific questions or concerns—something Winton credits for improved retention rates.

Collecting and analyzing data is easier and cheaper than you may think. Installing measurement tools—tools that tie membership engagement and action to financial return, like Google Analytics 360, which offers further analysis than previous iterations of Google Analytics—can help take the rest of your association's leadership from agnostics to advocates. Other, more customized, tools are also available to measure things you may have once thought unmeasurable. For example, Imagination has created a new tool called the Thought Leadership Index, which measures and assesses thought leadership achievement using five crucial data sets to determine whether you're achieving thought leadership success with your target audience.

Part III
Transfo

rmation

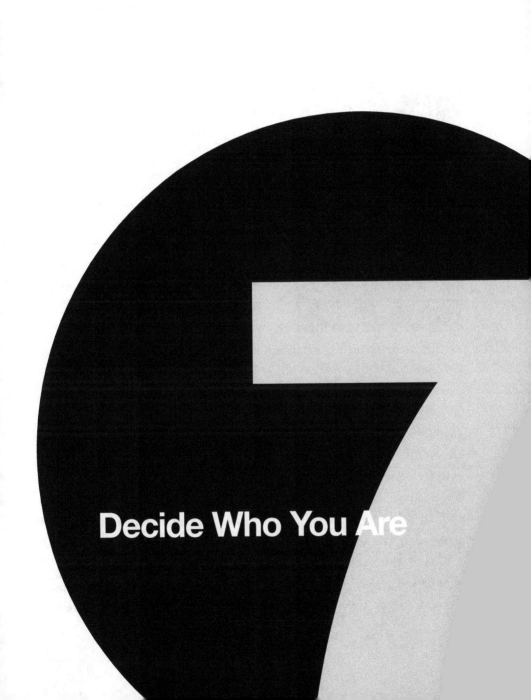

Decide Who You Are

"All of the services associations provide, members can pretty much get else-where. For a membership society to remain relevant and valuable, we need to be looking at what are the biggest issues in the discipline or the field."
—David Gammel, executive director, the Entomological Society of America

et's talk about the Girl Scouts. Its best-known fundraiser, baking and selling cookies, could easily be seen as anti-quated, a relic of an organization that's stuck in the past with outmoded notions of the worth and the role of women and girls. But no one thinks of Girl Scout cook-ies that way. That's not a coincidence. Rather than deride the cookies as something old fashioned, an anachronism, and shed them, the organiza-tion has modernized the program.

Any Girl Scout leader will tell you that the cookie sales are a means to engender financial literacy and business savvy. Today's Girl Scouts, as exemplified by its still hugely popular cookie sale, stands for something entirely contemporary: entrepreneurship and leadership. Here's how Girl Scouts currently characterizes its cookie sales: "As the largest entre-preneurial program for girls in the world, the Girl Scout Cookie Program is powering the next century of girl leaders toward an amazing future."

What a statement, from an organization that once required the girls to bake the cookies themselves.[36] Leadership and entrepreneurship are a new message for an old organization—a message that thousands of girls find compelling and empowering. "They're killing it," says MCI Group's Erin Fuller. "It's an old-school organization that's been smart and pivoted."

What's Your Story?

Every organization has a story, and that story changes over time. Your story is the reason you exist. It's your value proposition, but it doesn't take place in isolation. Stories that work, stories that resonate and connect, are placed in the context of the bigger world. It's what you're good for in the world. It's the reason people should care about you.

That big story—the thing that inspires people, inside and outside your organization—should give birth to a thousand smaller stories. Take the Girl Scouts. It's a huge organization with a broad membership. It has to appeal to girls—and their parents—of all backgrounds and locations. But its story is deceptively simple. Girl Scouts are training the next generation of leaders. Everything the organization does and says ladders up to that core story. Girl Scouts change the world, they volunteer, they start businesses, they get scholarships to college. Everything, at its base level, is about becoming leaders.

Once that story gels, it infuses the smaller stories the group tells every day about its members, giving each of those smaller stories a bigger platform and greater resonance. Girl Scouts are powerful. They excel in STEM. They fight injustice. Each girl's story becomes an embodiment of the organization's story and a way of demonstrating the organization's worth, energizing its members and driving interest from prospective members.

Every organization is capable of this. Remember the Entomological Society of America? Its story was about the vast, immediate, global impact of the discipline of entomology. By positioning itself that way, by having its events and its speakers positioned that way, the organization was thought of as a leader when a true crisis rolled around: the Zika virus. The organization's members were deliberately sought out as experts. "One of the big outcomes for that was to get the discipline elevated," says ESA's David Gammel.

Once you know what your association's story is, work on it. Refine it. Pressure test it against your strategic objectives. Once you're confident it's the right story, make sure every team and department knows what that story is. You've probably heard marketers hyping the importance of brand storytelling, to the point where your eyes roll skyward every time you hear it. And yet this vital skill of telling focused, engaging stories to attract, educate, entertain and retain members is beyond the grasp of many associations.

Your bigger story is going to engender a thousand derivative ones—member stories that aren't just designed to be warm and fuzzy celebrations of your members, but powerful endorsements of who you are as an organization and why you matter. "When you look at something like physiology, people don't understand its place in the world," says the American Physiological Society's Scott Steen. That's why, he says, part of his job is to make them understand—a story that gets back to universities and funders.

"I think the organizations that tell the story of their industry or profession well tend to succeed," he adds. It's worth noting, too, that it's not just science-based associations that have these kinds of stories. MCI Group's Fuller recalls working with client International Window Cleaning Association, a small trade association that represents window cleaners, especially those who clean large commercial buildings—the guys 40 stories in the air, washing office windows while strapped into a harness. Their story was a little ... boring, Fuller recalls.

Everything the organization does and says ladders up to that core story.

But once she dug in, she learned that window washers have a high rate of fatalities: about two people die each week cleaning windows. The group had a safety standard that was effective in reducing fatalities when used correctly. That

Takeaway: Your organization's story should engender a thousand smaller stories.

idea—safety—became the association's driving story. That shift in thinking changed how the group approached its storytelling and its marketing. Website imagery shifted from people sitting at conference tables to window washers suspended from buildings. The group shifted much of its focus to safety training—a more urgent message with a meaningful human connection.

You don't need to channel Stephen King to develop stories that drive results. All you need is to listen to your members to discover what topics and treatments they find fascinating—and are making a difference in the world. Think back to Steen's example in Chapter 6 of the scientists at the American Ceramic Society. There was the glass scientist who figured out how to encase nuclear waste in giant glass spheres that could be buried deep in the ground. There was the scientist who used his friend's liver cancer diagnosis as motivation to invent a more effective cancer treatment that uses microspheres of glass to isolate radiation to tumors within the liver.

Every association has members doing things that are an embodiment of its story. For a medical association, a successful story might be a podcast interview with a member who nailed a tricky diagnosis. Stories that work are appealing, interesting, enlightening, shocking, moving ... definitely not dull. They're on subjects that members are passionate about, that they need to know, that are relevant to their lives right now—and relevant to the broader world. Tap those stories for messaging gold.

Remember, too, that your organization may have multiple stories it's telling at once. Take CFP Board. One part of its story is to elevate the CFP credential. At the same time, the organization is also telling its story about creating a financial planner workforce that's more representative of the world—not just white men. That outward focus has helped the organization raise more than $10 million in funding for programs and research, Kevin Keller says.

This is not just promoting diversity because it's trendy. Keller is quick to note that a more diverse pool of financial planners, and promoting that effort, ladders up to the big goal of making the certification more broadly relevant and more valuable to its holders: It will elevate the profession.

Build the Right Brand

Your brand is notoriously hard to define. It's not a logo or a set of colors. It's not a slogan or a website. Your brand is all of those things and much more. Your brand is the embodiment of how people see you. It conveys a feeling, a vibe, a sense of who you are and what you stand for. Some people describe it as a promise—it's what you're going to offer your members and prospective members. Others, like the Project Management Institute's Cindy Anderson, vice president of brand management, describe it as the sum total of all the experiences someone has with your organization.

Right now you may be staring at your logo or your website, thinking that you have no idea what the heck it's promising or what it conveys. Maybe you're looking at a logo that's just an acronym, or something old-fashioned and typical of academic associations, like letters set against Greek-style columns. That's extremely common in the association world—but associations can't afford to give their brands short shrift any longer.

This is not fluffy marketing speak. Powerful brands—the ones that are carefully constructed and painstakingly executed—can make an organization. And they're not all huge organizations. Everyone knows what the Nike swoosh conveys. But I'm not talking about that. Think about Red Bull, about SoulCycle, about Dollar Shave Club. These are companies that started small and used the power of brand-building to convey their stories and build companies that people are obsessed with—truly sticky organizations. These are companies that know that their brand—the sum total of all the experiences their customer has—is the center of their organizations' power.

If you're not sure if your current brand is saying the right things, start at the beginning. Start with your association's story. Know that story inside and out. Think about why people should care about that story and how that story is going to connect with people—not just your staff, not just your members, but the broader community and even the public.

For many associations, thinking this way is a major shift. For decades, associations dispensed memberships and related products to a customer base that was practically a captive audience. Now, associations are forced to compete—in short, to position themselves much like for-profit companies in a crowded marketplace.

In the past, those running academic associations may have thought this line of thinking didn't apply to them—that their organizations were intended to be staid, to convey a kind of seriousness that renders branding irrelevant. That's no longer true. As subspecialties grow and blossom, and funding opportunities shrink, it's incumbent upon academic societies to be as forward-thinking about brand as other companies and groups. The American Mathematical Society realized that a few years ago when it looked at its logo—which looked like a Greek temple. The association changed it to be more contemporary, more vibrant, says Robert Harington. It's a reflection of the fact that "content hasn't changed, but the way we present it has," Harington says. The new logo—a swirl of dotted lines in three colors—"stresses how we are advancing research and creating connections."

Once you know those answers, you're closer to your brand. From here, to determine all the ways your brand can come to life, consider a touchpoint audit: Look at all of the ways and places people interact with your brand. That will include everything from your email signature to your website to your signage at events and the look and feel of your magazine. It's every way that your association touches people—all of the experiences your members and prospective members have.

Don't make the mistake, though, of thinking that a shiny new brand is all you need. "Sometimes an association—particularly when there's a change in leadership—wants to give it a fresh coat of paint and claim victory," says Sean McBride of DSM Strategic Communications. But a brand isn't a means to an end—it's part of a broader rethinking of where your organization fits in the world.

A touchpoint audit should consider all the places your members interact with your brand.

Events	Are people getting good content and making good connections? Is it generating buzz in the marketplace?
Website	Is it easy to navigate? Can you purchase simply? Is it easy to connect with other professionals?
Social media	Are posts current? Relevant? Are you commenting on other things that are important?
Product quality	Is the magazine giving information members can't get anywhere else? Is it helping members do their jobs better? Providing a means to make connections?
Chapter meetings	Are chapters growing? Getting publicity in local markets? Do they feel connected to the global brand? Leverage capabilities of the main office?

Indeed, Anderson says, while branding and marketing are incredibly powerful, they're not a substitute for a strategy. Says Anderson, "you need to be careful you don't just look at marketing and brand as the solution to a product set that doesn't make sense."

What's in a Name?

For many associations, rethinking your name is a natural place to start when you're considering a rebrand. Does your name really convey who you are? If your organization has been around for decades and decades, or if the field has changed (as so many have!) your name alone may be a turnoff for prospective members. Consider the Consumer Electronics

Association, which organizes the huge annual CES event in Las Vegas. In 2015, the Consumer Electronics Association announced a name change to the Consumer Technology Association (CTA), to reflect a membership base that had evolved beyond TV and computer makers to include companies like Lyft and Pandora. "The word 'electronics' is limiting and does not capture all the innovation swirling around wireless, the internet, automobiles, health and the new economy. The word 'technology' better defines what we have become and who we represent," CEO Gary Shapiro wrote in a blog post.[37]

That change also reflects the organization's evolution when it comes to its lobbying mandate—it represents the interests of a broad swath of technology companies.

There's one place CTA didn't update its naming convention: CES. The show has such broad name recognition and cachet that the association elected to leave that element as its own brand.

Not every name change is successful. In 2014, the National Speakers Association (NSA) announced it was changing its 40-year-old name to PLATFORM.[38] As reasons, the group said the word "association" was a bit stodgy, the group was no longer just "national," and its members did more than just "speak." So basically, the whole thing was obsolete, its branding consultant said. The new name and brand were intended to be "more inclusive."

The backlash was quick and fierce. Members complained that the process wasn't transparent and that the change was too dramatic and too sudden. Some people recoiled at the decidedly un-association-like name, saying it sounded like an event or a series, not like the name of a group. And, most problematic, NSA appeared not to have done sufficient research: the "Platform" name was already in use by a speaker and author to represent his book and educational events.

The upshot: The new name was a fail. NSA then-President Shep Hyken issued a video mea culpa, apologizing for the dramatic change and walking it back. "It's clear that we should have done a better job rolling

Does your name represent what you do in today's world?

out the brand to membership, and for that I do sincerely apologize," he said. He added that the group would go back to the drawing board and reconsider a brand that better addresses the association's membership and its needs. As of 2018, the old National Speakers Association name remained.

The lesson here is pretty clear: Be strategic. Remember that your members care about your name and your look—that brand, after all, represents who you are and a promise that members are affiliating with. That doesn't mean it doesn't need to be updated. It doesn't mean that you need to stick with the old naming convention that mandates that the word "association" be present—just look at powerful new associations like TechNet and the Self-Driving Coalition for Safer Streets.

It just means you should take the process seriously and engage all of your constituents. Remember, this is personal to a lot of people, especially longtime members. If you're struggling with your brand and aren't sure where to start, as usual, I recommend asking the people who matter most: your members and prospective members. Ask: How would you describe us? The answers are bound to fascinate and enlighten you.

But don't stop the questions there. After you develop your new name, you'll need to test it with members and prospective members. Put it out there and get your constituents' approval. Make sure you ease them into it: Build the case for change, give people the reason for it, and then introduce it in stages. By working through a multistep process, rather than a single unveiling, your members feel they've been heard, and they won't feel resentful of the change. "You can destroy the equity that's built up with members overnight by introducing a brand that's not accepted in the market," says Anderson.

Put the Customer First

At the most basic level, you are running a business. And that business has customers. Do you know who they are, and do you know what they want? Many associations, unfortunately, do not. "Eighty percent of association

Reality Check

Do you know your ...
renewal rate?

Lifetime value?

ROI on key
investments?

executives are likely running their organizations like nonprofits—no margin, no mission," says ASIS International's Peter O'Neil.

We've all heard the two most common excuses for that attitude: not enough staff and not enough resources. It's no excuse. "You never have enough staff and you have enough money," O'Neil says flatly. "Size does not matter. Run it like a business."

The first rule of any successful business is to know your customer. Putting your customer first will put you on the road to a suite of products and services that make sense—as well as a marketing strategy that effectively communicates the value of those products and services.

Designing a Strategy

Too often, associations spend many months and tens of thousands of dollars to come up with a strategic plan to address a membership slide or to become more innovative—and then that giant document, replete with months of blood, sweat and tears, turns into a doorstop.

To keep that from happening to you, start at the beginning—and picture the end. The most effective plans start by understanding why you're doing them. What are you trying to get out of the exercise? Are you looking to create large-scale change? Do you need to reconnect with your core constituency? Or are you trying to come up with ways to have a big impact on the world? The basic need should inform how you begin—this is the intelligence gathering phase.

Once you know the "why" of the exercise, you'll want to start with a few basic data points about your members and prospective members that every organization should know inside and out. This is the reality check that will tell you where you are today, so you know where you need to go next. Let's say, for example, your strategic plan is going to focus on membership. Before you build the strategy, you need the facts. You should know the details of your membership renewal rate. You should know the return on investment for your membership-building initiatives. And you should know both the cost of acquiring a member and the lifetime value of a member.

Profit you generate
from each member

X

Typical membership
length

=

Lifetime value (LTV)

If you see that your lifetime value is trending downward, that means you have a retention problem—or you're not making the most of members while you have them.

Having this basic set of metrics in place is critical to make your ongoing analysis easy and straightforward. If you're tracking on an ongoing basis, you'll quickly see trend lines around how much members are spending and over what period.

Sometimes, the strategic mission will be vast. When the Entomological Society of America set out to develop a strategic plan, the founding principles were broad, Gammel says:

1. The discipline of entomology is global; therefore so is ESA.
2. ESA must increase the influence of the discipline on society.
3. There's a social responsibility to influence society for all members.

From there, the theme grew to look beyond the association's typical horizons—to frame members' work in a more immediate and global context, to help them be more competitive for funding and raise their stature.

One really important note here: Members, Gammel says, weren't necessarily looking for that—because they wouldn't necessarily think to look to ESA for leadership in that area. But by building out a series of tactics against that strategy—the summits that looked at entomology's role in big, relevant areas like sustainable agriculture and climate change—the association set itself up as a leader, with new credibility in the public, the press, and ultimately among members and prospective members.

Your strategic plan may not be so vast. You may start smaller—like a plan to stanch a declining membership. You may discover, through that discovery process, that you're not communicating value to your members—a common problem among associations that are still publishing the same cocktail of a magazine, a member directory and some online content, without a differentiating value proposition.

That's what happened at the American Association of Sleep Technologists.[39] It had a vast library of content—but it wasn't being distributed in a meaningful way that connected with members. A blogging and

SEO strategy, with the help of marketing software provider HubSpot, increased traffic to the site. A social strategy distributed the content more efficiently and effectively. All content is tracked, as are leads collected on the site.

No matter what your strategic priorities are, the tactics should come *after* you build the initial strategy. The tactics—the social content, the summits, the discounts—are how you accomplish the plan. But you can't decide what those tactics are until you know what the bigger strategy is.

Listen to Your Members

Chances are, at some early point in developing your strategic plan, you will want to talk to your members and maybe prospective members, too. Dare I say it: This is not associations' strong suit. Sure, you probably do a member survey every few years, and maybe you've updated some of the questions. But when it comes to strategic planning, many association executives believe they know everything there is to know about their members.

That's a failure-making attitude in an era of rapid change. It's always worth the time to talk to the people who are paying your bills. For small organizations—even for big ones!—there are incredibly easy ways to do this. SurveyMonkey and other similar software is low-cost, and deployment takes just minutes. Ask questions in your social media feeds to get a quick response—and engage your members at the same time.

If you've never gone through the exercise of creating personas, now is a great time to start. Begin by distilling what you know about your members. How old are they? Where do they live? Where are they in their careers?

Don't forget psychographics—those personal characteristics that will help you create relevant, compelling content. What are their

Ask: On a scale of 1 to 10, how likely are you to recommend us to a colleague or fellow professional?

How Much Do You Love Me? Understanding Net Promoter Scores

As you're crafting your questions, there's one big one I recommend: the net promoter score. Net promoter score (NPS) is essentially an index that reveals how likely your customers or members are to recommend you. It's a proxy for members' satisfaction.

Asking a question about likelihood to recommend is critically important because those who are dissatisfied with you are far more likely to tell other people than those who are satisfied. So how do you calculate your NPS? Ask: On a scale of 1 to 10, how likely are you to recommend us to a colleague or fellow professional?

Those who answer with a 9 or 10 are your promoters—the ones who are likeliest to recommend. A 7 or 8 indicates a more neutral stance, known as "passives." Respondents who select 0 through 6 are "detractors," those who likely wouldn't recommend you.

To calculate your NPS, subtract the percentage of detractors from the percentage of promoters.

If you asked 100 members, and:

- 70 were Promoters
- 10 were Passives
- 20 were Detractors

Your NPS is 50.

Is 50 good? Different industries have different average scores. You definitely want to be in positive territory. Generally, an NPS above 50 indicates you're in great shape with your members. If the readout is negative, you've got work to do.

primary and secondary needs? Pain points? Think back to early career nurses and the pervasiveness of bullying in the workplace—a significant insight that led to a successful, impactful content program. Dig for nuggets around behavior, attitudes, motivations behind behavior and unmet needs that can help you tailor your programming. While you have a single value proposition as an organization, how you deliver that value may vary for each persona you're talking to.

Don't forget about your prospects. If your goal isn't just to deepen relationships with existing members, but to increase your pipeline of new members, then you must develop personas for those prospective members, too. In doing so, you may just uncover some of the reasons you've been missing the mark with them.

8

Architect the Experience

"When you run around after margin, you inadvertently lose sight of the mission." —Peter O'Neil, CEO, ASIS International

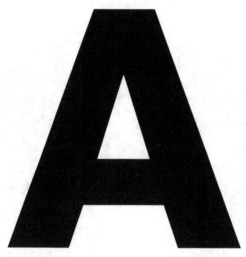

fter all of this—thinking about relevance, about mission, about who you are and who you're talking to—how do you put a plan into motion at your organization? You can break down your plan into four steps: membership, content, experiences and people. First, you want to build the membership structure that makes the most sense for your audience. Next, you want to invest in the content that differentiates you. Third, you'll need to design memorable, meaningful experiences. And finally, your organization should make the most of your members—for your benefit and theirs.

Make Membership Valuable—Or Eliminate It

This is probably the biggest project you have to tackle to futureproof your association. The million-dollar question: What is the membership structure that makes the most sense for you—the one that is true to your mission, delivers the most value and is sustainable?

Start with your value as an association. The meaning of "value" now fluctuates depending on each member's location, age group and reason for joining your association. And while membership isn't dead, it's definitely not the center of life that it used to be, not least because the world is full of free and low-cost "memberships."

Once you have all of your data points and your personas, consider who you are and your place in the world. If you think about all of the people I've mentioned in this book, their structures work because they know exactly who they are. At ASIS, for example, Peter O'Neil knows that there is a core constituency that still believes deeply in affiliating—and others who simply want the magazine. That's why, he says, the organization is likely to move toward a tiered membership model rather than the current, $195 per year, take-it-or-leave-it model.

That's very different than AIIM, where Peggy Winton realized a few years back that the organization would be best off serving a broader community of nonmembers. Today, AIIM's model is essentially a hybrid program, with a traditional full-service membership track and a "freemium" track. In that case, the subscribers become a market to sell to. If you go this route, remember that information is gold. When you collect personal information, for a download or access to a webinar, the fewer fields you require, the more likely you are to get sign-ups. You might consider a form that asks for just five elements: first name, last name, company, ZIP code and email. That's all you need to know where they are and to have a way of contacting them.

The reality, notes MCI Group's Erin Fuller, is that devoting energy to a nonmember, freemium program may make much more sense than throwing buckets of money at traditional member services—especially if membership makes up less than 30 percent of your revenue. There are some industries, too, where it makes more sense than others, such as those where professionals are continually changing companies and jobs, like media, or where consolidation is rampant. Trying to keep up with a membership base that's constantly on the move can be hugely expensive.

A big, qualified database not only allows you a bigger market to sell products and services to—it can help you secure money-making

What you don't want:

Motion without progress

What you do want:

Evolutionary change

partnerships. AIIM's partner vendors may pay $15,000 to be an exclusive, participating sponsor of a webinar because of the huge database that they are able to access.

The possibilities are broad. Many associations are moving toward a tiered model, with an entry price point, a mid-price point and a higher, or premium, price point with additional benefits. Others are looking at hybrid structures where a certain number of staffers are covered when an individual or company joins. Giving access to a broader base can make sense when you're building out a patchwork model of different products and services that may appeal to different audiences. And yet, far too many associations are still pushing old- school, one-size-fits-all "benefits."

If you don't have the research at your fingertips, the most obvious strategy is to survey your members to find out what they want that you aren't providing ... and then provide it. Or even better, as I keep saying, get out there and talk to your members. Remember CFP Board? Kevin Keller was able to increase membership fees—almost doubling them!—because the association doubled down on its mission to make CFP certification a must-have designation.

You can also increase the impact of your *current* offerings by allowing members to customize how their value equation is set up—which of your association's benefits and information they receive and how and when they receive them.

It doesn't matter how personalized a member's benefits package is, though, if the member doesn't understand what those benefits are and how to use them. A survey of first-year members of the National Federation of Independent Business, for example, showed that members who use just one of an association's services have a 16 percent higher renewal rate.

Make sure you're not missing simple diagnoses to your membership problems. Marketing General's Tony Rossell notes that in his work with associations, often lapsed members will say they simply "forgot" to renew. That should never happen! "Something's wrong with your renewal system if 30 percent of people didn't even know they lapsed,"

3 components of a futureproofed membership structure

Rossell says. So dig in to the data. Are you using multiple channels to reach out? Reaching out often enough?

Got clueless members? See if you've got a big group of members who aren't opening emails or other communications. If so, boost their awareness and understanding of the value your association provides through tools such as instructional videos, group orientation calls, SlideShare tutorials, monthly tip emails aimed directly at benefits and how-to posts with screenshots that outline steps for using your association's resources and tools.

Elevate Your Content

I talked earlier about doubling down on content that matters. What that means will differ for every organization, but when you do it right, it's game-changing, the way the bullying survival series was for ANA and the way the "cluster" content was for the Hudson Valley Economic Development Corp. To get to your game-changing content, start by thinking of your competitive advantage. Maybe you can provide newer, faster, better content and products than your competitors. Or perhaps your focus is on depth rather than speed, and you can package your insider POV and information as added value. Or combine content, services and products in a counterintuitive way that actually works.

You don't want to try to compete with the faux thought leaders who are tweeting platitudes by the hour. Your value is proven expertise and the ability to curate what really matters. Provide true insider viewpoints that members can't get elsewhere for free—because

If you can make sense of uncertainty and lead on changes and trends, you will be the trusted source that stands head and shoulders above the cacophony of content makers.

Proven expertise

+

relentless relevance

=

content that matters

the insiders you choose are those whose expertise is too valuable to spread around gratis. Remember the expression "You get what you pay for"? Make that your motto. Make quality count.

You may have already created realistic, exhaustive member personas that include members' demographics, motivations, needs, pain points and lifestyles. Well done: This savvy move forces you to look at your association through the point of view of your members. But creating content that resonates with all your member personas, and delivering it in the way they prefer, can be a daunting task. Personalization is key to creating messaging that matters, but how can you keep it from taking over your workday?

Robb Lee, chief marketing and communications officer of the ASAE, The Center for Association Leadership, suggests breaking the cycle of overwhelm by analyzing the personas you develop to find the commonalities instead of the differences among your members.

For example, if you're a trade organization, maybe your members need shareable content that showcases the value of what they do. Or, if most of your members are smack in the middle of their member journey, maybe they need information that will help them rise to the top of their profession. Understanding the threads that connect all your members can help your association wrap its collective head around members' greatest wants and needs—and develop the content that matters most.

Remember, you can create all kinds of content, and if what you've been doing is still resonating with members, that's great—keep doing it. But the association of the future has the duty to recognize and call out the trends that may be affecting members and prospective members—often before they realize it. If you can make sense of uncertainty and lead on changes and trends, you will be the trusted source that stands head and shoulders above the cacophony of content makers.

Once you've done that, the big difference in how you serve each member persona may lie in the delivery of the content. A message created to appeal to a broad range of members might multitask, with strategic tweaking, as an article in a print magazine, a podcast interview with an expert, a blurb in an email newsletter, a listicle on LinkedIn, a teaser on Twitter and an Instagrammed photo that's worth a thousand words—each reaching a different member persona in the way that works best for them.

To increase the personalization of your content delivery even more, allow members to choose between a daily email and a weekly digest; to opt in to instant text notifications for breaking news; and to choose what information appears when they visit your website's member portal, depending on their needs and their point in the member journey.

Also, keep in mind that many outside sources offering free content are only working one channel. Use your resources to create omnichannel content so each member can get information the way he or she wants it—from print to podcasts to Instagram.

Doing this effectively requires investing in data: You can't give people what they want if you don't know what that is. Remember Marketing General's Rossell's insight that as many as 90 percent of associations have no idea the age of anyone in their database. You should be striving not just to understand member age, but also their preferences. Without real data insights, you can't differentiate effectively.

For more on the practice, flip to Chapter 9, where I talk about building data into every day.

The way content gets delivered is naturally a bit different for academic societies that are built around a journal publishing model—but not as different as you might think. While the content is less commercial by nature, many forward-thinking academic association leaders, like the AMS's Robert Harington, are rethinking the journal model beyond its traditional roots. Rather than retreat to barebones, the strategy is to publish more—and publish more broadly, into more general interest content. That's why the organization pursued the purchase of a more general interest publisher and absorbed its content.

Those kinds of moves, though, can be difficult for some boards of directors to wrap their heads around. When it comes to the board, "there's a natural suspicion of being too businesslike," Harington says. Over the years, he adds, he has learned to navigate that tension by being careful to curb the marketing and business speak when he's presenting to the board—while still instilling the urgency of making changes to the model. "I can tell them what the business requirements are, and they can say where to balance. But if you're too idealistic, the business suffers."

When I talk about consistent messaging, it's essential to acknowledge that a style that works for one format can't be dropped as-is into another. A long-form article in an association's print magazine becomes a 140-character pull quote on Twitter. A 60-minute video tutorial becomes a paragraph-long blurb with a link in the email newsletter. This is only natural due to the differences in style and user expectations among the platforms themselves. Members won't bat an eye when a hard-hitting pull quote on Twitter becomes an introspective long-form article in the print magazine or when a breezy email blurb morphs into an in-depth video lesson. They'll admire the consistency.

This is an essential part of the content execution plan—getting the most from everything you produce. It makes your content cheaper, more efficient and more impactful—because you reach people who interact on different channels. AIIM's Winton notes that every piece of content the association produces gets reused about five ways. Got some interesting data? It can be turned into a report. At AIIM, paid members might get the raw data points as well as a slide deck. Those who don't pay may be able to access a free executive summary, an infographic and a webinar. The webinar replay might live on YouTube, and the whole package could yield dozens, even hundreds, of social posts.

That's the way to make the most of your content.

Design Meaningful Experiences

Red Bull is known as the company that created the energy drink category. But when you visit the front page of its website, energy drinks are nowhere to be seen.

Instead, the company plasters its website with Red Bull-produced events like 3-on-3 basketball tournaments, cliff diving competitions and music festivals, plus stunning videos of its sponsored athletes at work and play. This is a company that takes its slogan seriously and makes participants feel like they have "wings." Note that none of those experiences are directly about energy drinks. Instead, they all bring life to Red Bull's slogan—to give you wings.

You don't have to be a hip energy-drink company to use this mission-first strategy. You don't have to be a huge organization, either. Any association can create membership experiences that reflect its mission and offer incredible member value. For example, the International Interior Design Association recently moved into a 17,000-square-foot space that lets the association hold member training and education events on-site. "It's an incredibly well-designed space, which makes meetings easier to manage," says CEO Cheryl Durst. "People wonder sometimes when they sit in a typical board room why everyone is tired and exhausted. A poorly designed space that doesn't consider the occupants will make a two-hour meeting seem like a six-hour meeting." Design association + well-designed meeting space = mission (statement) accomplished.

Don't for a second think that you should be eschewing events—or taking everything online. There is no substitute for the power of the human connection, says Pat Cleary, President and CEO of the National Association of Professional Employer Organizations (NAPEO). In fact, in-person networking remains one of associations' critical differentiators. "We pack content into conferences when what people want to do is talk to each other. Over and over, our evaluations say, 'Let us network!' What they want is to talk to each other."

That's the power of an association, especially one that's specialized. Cleary notes that, "If you have a specific PEO question, you can go to a thousand SHRM (Society for Human Resource Management) conferences and not find an answer. But you'll find it from one of our members at one of our conferences."

Events are often a safe space for professionals in your industry, one where they can network with competitors and have exchanges that just can't happen anywhere else. The question becomes how you should focus and design your events.

Any association that holds an annual conference should be considering whether that event is due for a refresh. Times change, and there's no question that the traditional trade show model, with its floor of vendor booths and roster of speakers, is under duress. That's why ASIS evolved its annual event to include exclusive events on the trade show floor—events that will literally be held behind a curtain. The association also rebranded the event, to the Global Security Exchange. There's just no room for the same-old-same-old events.

As always, the strategy for your event should come back to your mission, your reason for being. That's how David Gammel at ESA decided to pursue a series of summits on critical global issues—issues that would elevate the discipline and get entomologists noticed. That's why the Hudson Valley Economic Development Corp. found great success with its "Disrupted" event, which featured the founder of Foursquare talking about the dynamics of the modern economy. HVEDC was a trusted source of information on the future of the economy—information it was delivering in a new and dynamic way—a way that would lead area entrepreneurs to see HVEDC as a leader in the space. The more you can create differentiating, difference-making events, the more your audience will trust your voice.

There's another unifying thread in these successful, updated events, and that's the idea of a common experience. In the social media era, everyone wants to feel like they have something worth sharing and commenting on. Real-life experiences have become, in many ways, even more important. When you give people something to hold onto—an experience that turns into a hashtag, whether it's a social media hashtag or just a single memory worth clinging to—they want to come back, and they want to talk about it.

An association for association execs needs to be out front, taking risks and experimenting big with processes and initiatives. One of those initiatives for ASAE was the 2016 first Xperience Design Project (XDP), a show for association professionals and industry partners who plan, build or support association events. We all know how millennials are leery of staid conferences and dull trade shows. XDP's mission was to "redefine how trade shows, conferences and events are created and delivered." The schedule included a collaborative learning experience called The Lab; LabX, which featured TED-style recaps of key ideas; the Business Exchange, a marketplace of industry partners; and, yeah, a private B-52s concert.

"It's important that members look to us to try new things in order to help inform what they should and should not be doing ... which by definition means that we should be trying to do new and different things and sharing the outcomes," says ASAE's Lee. "XDP was a tremendous win for us."

The idea of creating a common experience may not feel all that different to you, but it's a notable shift. The problem with many of today's conferences and trade shows is that they don't feel all that different from a webinar—and that's not going to get people there. "The human parts are really, really important," says the American Physiological Society's Scott Steen. "But the delivery of them has to be different." Today's events must feel like a hub—they must operate like the center of something. If your members can get practically the same content virtually—they are simply not going to show up.

Let Your Members Shine

Your members are looking outside the association for expert news and advice, while by definition your association is full of experts. Why not give your members the opportunity to ask one another questions and to show off their own smarts and skills?

This is one of associations' key differentiators: Don't try to compete with your members. Instead, elevate them and facilitate their successes.

This is something they can't get anywhere else—the ability to be broadly recognized by their peers.

In 2014, the American Association for Clinical Chemistry launched an online member community called AACC Artery that does just that. The Artery allows members to post questions—such as "How can I solve this problem I'm having in my lab?"—and, within hours, receive dozens of helpful replies from fellow members.

This is just one of the ways that associations can curate content. In a marketplace crowded with people offering their opinions—in social media, online, everywhere they can—you have the ability to leverage the inherent trust members have in the association. Facilitating helpful connections and problem-solving information is a way of combatting the commoditization of information.

"It has been a huge success. Huge," says Molly Polen, AACC's senior director of communications and public relations. In 2016 AACC conducted an extensive survey to identify drivers of member retention, and the Artery was at the top of the list.

Similarly, AIIM has launched a virtual "VIP lounge" with events for premium members. Members can reach out for help on a specific issue, and the organization will set up a so-called peer-to-peer brain date to solve the problem. "It's based on what people tell us they need," says AIIM's Winton. "I can't help but think that's the reason we're seeing improved retention."

Publicizing your members' successes is another sure way to gain their loyalty. "We tout our members on Facebook and Twitter," says NAPEO's Cleary. "We get a ton of activity on our Twitter page. Rather than undermining us, social media has given us another outlet to champion our members. One of our members just wrote a management book. We promoted it on Twitter and got a lot of traffic, a lot of attention he couldn't have gotten another way."

Publicizing and supporting your members' breakthrough work is beneficial for them and for you. As I talked about in Chapter 4, funders and politicians follow public opinion. The more you're getting your members out there and recognized, the greater the ripple effect will be—with the ultimate effect of raising the clout of the profession.

Awards have historically been an important way for associations to let their members shine—and they continue to be. But if you haven't revisited your awards portfolio in a few years, now is the time to do it. So many fields are changing so quickly—your awards submissions offer clues to what's relevant and what's not. ESA, for example, underwent an exercise to update its portfolio of awards—creating new ones in different disciplines and winding down the ones that weren't working.

Don't forget the opportunity to include your members in your own initiatives, as AGU did when it created the open API challenge. The organization got great ideas for making meetings more relevant and exciting, and its members got enhanced visibility and a shot at a little cash.

For any kind of awards program, the metrics are simple: If you're only getting a few submissions, it's probably no longer important to the future of your field. Take the time to consider your awards program and evolve it so forward-looking member work is getting the right spotlight.

Build the Right Organization

"Struggling associations are generally really bad at marketing."
—Tony Rossell, senior vice president, Marketing General Inc.

ow what? It's time to build an organization that makes membership matter, produces compelling content and experiences, and elevates its members and the profession. Getting there begins by understanding the internal pressures you face—rather than simply continuing to operate as you always have.

In this way, associations may face their toughest test: Unlike big public companies with activist investors, it's easier for association leadership to bury their heads in the sand in the face of pressures. When that happens, the organization continues to operate as it always has, making true change impossible.

To become the association of the future, your culture and your organization need to reflect those priorities. Here's how to get there.

Clean House

You knew this was coming, right? Associations have a long-standing reputation for being the landing spot for professionals who want the easy, slow road to retirement. Maybe this isn't your organization. But chances are, it is—at least in some departments.

Every successful association executive I interviewed for this book had a story to tell about positioning the staff to move into the future. In many cases, it wasn't pretty, but it was necessary.

Organizational culture is the single biggest issue ASIS International's Peter O'Neil has dealt with as the leader of several associations. "Culture eats strategy for lunch," he says. Nothing can get done if you don't have the right people in place.

"When you allow people to sit in their offices and retire—I rebel against that," he adds. "It ends up being your undoing."

Where to begin? Start by simply considering that you want to work with the best people you can. When O'Neil began his role at ASIS, he met with almost every staff member, asking questions about who was difficult to work with and who was an impediment to organizational progress. Five common names came up over and over again; those were the first five people he let go. If this task feels too herculean or you think some fresh eyes could be beneficial, this is a great time to consider bringing on an outside consultant to help jump-start change, as PMI did. An outside group can be a catalyst for building a leaner, more efficient, more modern operation.

When Scott Steen came in from the outside and took the helm at American Forests, everyone knew things weren't good—the organization had shed $3 million in funding the previous nine months—but the board didn't know quite how bad it had gotten. Steen remembers noticing a man sitting in the lobby, not doing much. He asked who it was and was told, "That's Eddie, our mailroom supervisor."

Except the organization didn't do mailings anymore. Eddie had turned into the guy you called when you wanted a bookcase moved, or something similar. Eddie was being paid $60,000 a year.

That's an incredibly common scenario at associations, though not all irrelevant or superfluous roles will be as obvious as Eddie's. Some

The mantra:

I will …
commit to innovation

I will …
act more nimble

I will …
clean house

I will …
hire experts and get the hell out of the way

workers are simply toxic, and many have been able to park at associations for years, even decades. Those are the ones to focus on first.

O'Neil says he likes to think about the "how"—how the work gets done day in and day out. The people who sit in their offices, unwilling to collaborate, simply have to go. While firing people is never easy, O'Neil says, as the leader of an organization, "it gives you a lot of credibility when you let people go who should have been let go 20 years ago. My profession allows too many people the option to be like government workers."

AIIM's Peggy Winton, you may recall, tells all of her staff that they're not in the association business—they're in the marketing business. That doesn't necessarily sit well with legacy staff who were brought on with a decidedly different mindset. She knew early on, she says, that not everyone was going to be willing to go along with this new vision. To make the transition as easy as possible, she says, she's been candid from the beginning on the direction she was taking the association. "I've tried to make it easy for certain folks to go on and do different things if they don't see themselves in this vision."

In a few cases, she says, she made an effort to reach out to staffers and acknowledge that she was aware they were no longer happy. In those cases, she offered to help the workers find their next opportunity; they often took her up on it.

Let Information Flow

When an association's messaging is "owned" by its leadership, and each department below the C-suite works in its own little bubble, it

"It gives you a lot of credibility when you let people go who should have been let go 20 years ago. My profession allows too many people the option to be like government workers."

Who's on First? How Digital First and Audience First Come Together

I've talked a lot about game-changing programming and content, the kind that's driven by what your audience wants. But you can't reach peak relevance—and peak stickiness—unless everything that you do is delivered to your audience where they are, how they want it. In short, you need to think audience first.

Audience first means a lot of things. It means understanding that your members and prospective members want information presented on their terms, not yours. It means understanding their mindset and their triggers and constantly listening and evolving. And for many organizations, it means shifting to a digital-first mentality, because that's where your audience is.

This isn't going to be true to the same degree for every organization. The first step is to know how your audience consumes information and programming: Your personas should help you with this. Once you understand how your users consume information, you can tailor your offerings accordingly. After all, you'll be incredibly frustrated if you create impactful, resource-intensive content and programming and then put it on a website no one visits.

Digital first is a new way of thinking. It allows you to produce more quickly, be more responsive to audience need, and be more responsive to data. But getting there takes a full-throated commitment. AGU is partway down that road. The association is working toward a platform that will allow users to see the content they want, customized to them, via an app.

Rather than see content organized by categories like upcoming meetings and journals and news, content will be organized around discipline-related topics—maybe "manmade hazards" or "planetary science." Once a user signs up for a topical feed, they'll receive relevant updates that could include any type of content. Eventually, AGU plans to add curated content as well. Today, a user who's interested in a certain topic has to go to the online library to find related journal content and check the meeting agendas to see if there are sessions on that topic, says Chris McEntee. The new digital-first strategy will change all of that, delivering whatever information people are interested in on whatever device they're using.

It's a labor-intensive process, McEntee says, and one of the hardest aspects is changing how the internal staff thinks about what they're working on and producing every day. "We're changing so everyone in the department is thinking about the entire person," she says. "The biggest challenge is changing how people work."

shows. If your newsletters read like business memos, but your tweets read like TMZ headlines, there's a disconnect.

When there's a disconnect, your editorial isn't the only thing that suffers. In many organizations, there's a tendency for each team to focus on its own goals, with those smaller accomplishments taking precedence over the bigger picture.

The fix? First, stop thinking in terms of product-based teams or department needs. Instead, come back to the customer-first mentality. When everyone is focused on what the customer and prospective customer needs, the silos should naturally drop away.

Then, weed out the people who just can't work this way. We all know these people—the ones who write a great report but don't put the information in the database or who can't work as part of a team. Those people undermine a movement toward a collective goal.

This goes for your senior staff too, says O'Neil. He practices what he calls the "one voice" culture. That means making sure that senior staff are all presenting the same story, all the time. That doesn't mean that everyone agrees all the time, of course. But O'Neil says that when he and the senior team meet, they "don't leave the room until we agree, and sometimes we agree to disagree." A one-voice philosophy encourages the entire staff to work together toward something common. Otherwise, O'Neil says, "they all turn on each other."

Once you have the right team in place, work on your story and make sure every team and department knows what that story is. Encourage a free flow of information and ideas among different departments so that everyone involved in messaging—which is everyone in the association, by the way—is on the same wavelength when it comes to the association's core purpose and the tone and style of its communications.

A forum on your association intranet or an intraoffice task group can give employees a platform to brainstorm ideas, discuss current projects, and ensure that messaging is consistent among different departments and channels. Another strategy: Develop a style guide that outlines the association's story and its preferred communication do's and don'ts. Then make it required reading for all your employees.

Build Innovation Into Every Day

Innovation is a popular talking point at associations these days, and with good reason: If you can't think differently or innovatively, your prospects are not good. The world is moving too fast to keep doing what you've been doing, the way you've been doing it.

Innovation is easy to talk about and hard to implement—particularly if your association is populated by lots of longtime employees who are used to doing things a certain way. To build a culture of innovation, work in stages. For the National Business Aviation Association (NBAA), building a more innovative organization is a concerted, multiyear process—the association isn't all the way through it yet.

First, lay the groundwork. That first year, the organization made an effort to understand where it stood in the universe of innovation. It looked at its own culture and the impediments it had in its people and processes. In that phase, leaders issued an internal survey asking employees how they thought the organization could be more innovative.

With the internal research under its belt, in year two, NBAA looked outside its own walls. The association wanted to compare itself to other, similar, organizations. The problem, says NBAA's Chris Strong, was that the organization couldn't find any sort of innovation benchmarking in the association space. So, working with Marketing General, NBAA staff created a survey asking what other organizations were doing to innovate. The survey went out to 150 companies, and NBAA heard back from half of those. When the organization compared its own processes and culture to the results, "that told us where we were on the spectrum," Strong says.

To truly transform, it was crucial that the idea of innovation had buy-in from the top of the organization all the way through the ranks, Strong notes. Innovation has become an association-wide goal. And that's not just lip service. Every employee is responsible for looking at what they do and coming up with their own innovation goal. On his office wall, Strong says, he has listed the six innovation-related things he's supposed to accomplish this year.

Upper management knew that not everyone would come up with an innovation goal and just go off and achieve it. They built out an infrastructure to support the greater goal of innovation. Some of the changes are cultural: NBAA has an innovation book club, where whoever wants to participate collectively chooses an innovation-related book to read and discuss. The organization periodically brings in innovation-related speakers. Other changes are more material: Each employee will be measured on his or her personal innovation goals—innovation has become a metric that's part of employees' annual reviews.

Strong is quick to admit that not all of the changes have been smooth sailing. Particularly for lower-level staff, having a manager who encourages new ideas was critical. To circumvent the potential for managers who might be lukewarm on a particular idea or the process overall, one idea was to start an innovation committee made up of seven members of the senior staff. Staffers could submit an idea via a web link and it would go to the innovation committee for consideration. Nothing meaningful has come out of that yet, Strong says.

Here's a simple tweak associations can make, one that will lead to bigger changes: Gather your staff to conduct thought experiments. For example, in his book *Originals: How Non-Conformists Move the World*, author Adam Grant suggests challenging employees to come up with ideas that will "make the company" (opportunities) and ideas that might "break the company" (risks your competitors and the marketplace pose to your organization). Then, you and your team brainstorm solutions to proactively innovate and solve for those risks, and make plans to put your solutions into place now.

Bringing departments together has the effect of breaking down silo walls just a little; thought experiments help shake staff members out of complacency; and brainstorming as a team gets everyone invested in the resulting ideas, breaking down resistance to implementation. This small tweak to your M.O. might lead to major changes, such as overhauling your content strategy or recognizing that your message isn't just national, it's global.

Fail Fast or Fail Slow?

The only way to avoid being left in the dust is to speed up to match the pace of change.

Taking fast action is hard when you're immersed in an association culture that's hesitant to make important decisions without dotting every i and crossing every t. Policies must be in place! Rules must be adhered to! Compliance must be consulted! Benchmarks (that were set 20 years ago) must be met!

The issue with that: Certainty is never guaranteed. If you wait to take action until you're 100 percent certain of the outcome, you'll keep on playing catch-up, something today's associations simply can't afford.

It's been years since association leadership started talking about operating like a business. Today, that isn't enough. What if you take a page out of the Silicon Valley playbook and move ahead with initiatives when you're 80 percent or 90 percent sure of the outcome? This moderate-but-tolerable amount of uncertainty is a natural part of the risk-opportunity equation. In the business world, companies that rule the market are those that have a healthy amount of risk tolerance, because they know there is no advancement without risk. For example, the internet is littered with lists of Amazon's famous failures—from the Fire Phone to Amazon Destinations—yet Amazon is one of the largest and fastest-growing companies on the planet.

Or consider Google. The company runs an entire division—called X— devoted to what it terms "moonshots." Those are almost impossibly big questions like: Can balloons deliver internet to remote corners of the world? Can kites be used to generate electricity?[40] The division is devoted to pursuing these kinds of game-changing ideas.

You can't explore these questions without building a culture that embraces failure, notes Astro Teller, who runs the division.[41] In fact, it's all about failing as quickly as possible: a strategy that ensures that the projects that stick around are the ones that are the most viable. In a TED talk, Teller says, "we spend most of our time breaking things and trying to prove that we're wrong." By constantly trying to come up with ways their projects might not work—enthusiastic skepticism—he calls it, the team determines what to leave on the cutting room floor. It's a culture that embraces failure from the outset.

There's a good reason for that: It's efficient. "If there's an Achilles heel in one of our projects, we want to know it now," says Teller—not millions of dollars into development.

Building a culture that's safe for failure takes concerted effort. Failing is not something most people want to do. You have to make failure feel okay, if not good. "You cannot yell at people and force them to fail fast. People resist. They worry, what will happen to me if I fail? Will people laugh at me? Will I be fired?" That's natural. That's why, at X, staffers are rewarded for failure. They're promoted and recognized. In short, "we make it safe to fail," Teller says.

A note of caution here: Experimentation for the sake of it is not what I'm advocating. I'm not saying that associations should be just like Google. Associations don't have the money, the resources or the stomach for that kind of operation. Change is exciting, but it can also be dangerous when it's not executed carefully. "Best practices dictate evolutionary change" for associations, says DSM's Sean McBride. Don't fall into the trap of motion without progress—change for the sake of it—which can cost time and money and end up draining morale.

But a slight shift toward a more failure-friendly mindset can be incredibly beneficial for organizations that historically have been cautious and plodding—a mindset a hyper-competitive world simply no longer supports.

That means you have to both require your staff to innovate and reward them for it. It also means moving closer to a fail-fast culture, so you don't squander untold amounts of money and time on projects that ultimately won't succeed. One approach that works for some organizations is something that management guru Peter Drucker called "purposeful abandonment." Every leader must know when it's time to sunset something, to admit it didn't live up to expectations and stop throwing good money after bad. That ability is crucial for any association looking to incorporate more innovative ideas into its mix.

Represent the Future

You can't build an organization that's positioned to grow a young and more diverse membership unless that customer base is represented within your own walls. And when I say represented, I don't mean that you're simply hiring recent grads to run your social media feeds.

Hiring—and listening to—younger staffers can go a long way toward connecting with that audience. A few years ago, says NBAA's Strong, a 20-something staffer approached him and said the organization wasn't doing a very good job engaging millennials. Strong, in turn, asked her to come up with some ideas as part of her job goals.

The woman gathered a few millennial staffers from different departments—marketing, trade shows, communications—and together they decided to form a young professionals' organization among membership. The first year, that young professional group sponsored a meet and greet at the trade show floor at the annual conference. They marketed a meetup for drinks. A few people showed up; they considered it a success.

The next year, they expanded the offering. Rather than just drinks, they put together a panel of young professionals talking about next steps for their careers. Despite a 9:30 a.m. start time—in Las Vegas of all places—150 people showed up, Strong remembers. Before long, vendors began to surface unprompted, offering to pay $10,000 to sponsor a young professionals segment or event at future shows.

Next up, the group is planning to launch a mentorship program. The whole young professional networking idea "has just blown up," says

Strong—a clear indication that that segment was out there, just waiting to be engaged with in the right way. As an organization, "we're as close to that [millennial] group as we've gotten."

Plus, he adds, he doesn't think it's unrelated that since then none of the young staffers have quit their jobs at NBAA.

You can't talk about the future without talking about diversity. Many leading associations are out in front on this issue—taking a stand on making a profession more representative of the world around us, the way the Ohio Society of CPAs is through its diversity and inclusion initiatives. But that's not enough. Don't forget about diversity within your own walls.

You can't represent the future of a profession unless that future is exemplified within your organization. Study after study has shown that people need to see themselves reflected in the path they choose. Having a diverse workforce will benefit both your organization and your members.

Take the American Society of Association Executives. ASAE understands millennials' quest for meaning—and also the fact that just about every member appreciates experiences that matter and policies that promote diversity and inclusion.

In 2012, ASAE developed a Diversity and Inclusion (D&I) case statement—which includes a glossary of terms and a convincing list of reasons to start a D&I program—to help associations get started with their own D&I initiatives. The association also offers the Association Inclusion Index, a self-testing tool to assess D&I policies and objectives against validated benchmarks.

It comes down to this: If you do not have diverse perspectives on your team, your organization will not be relevant in our changing world, says OSCPA's Scott Wiley.

Be Efficient and Accountable

Once you've made the decision to change up your association's messaging, the next challenge is to get the work done as efficiently as possible. It is difficult for any established company to operate efficiently. Legacy systems take hold, relationships are established and cemented, processes become gospel. To make a meaningful change, efficiency has to be addressed. As everyone who leads an association knows, there will never be enough money, and there will never be enough resources. To make the most of what you have, you must be as efficient as possible.

Efficiency is partly about having the right people in place, as I've already talked about. You're never going to make great, meaningful strides if you have toxic employees—or if you have a staff full of people who are only willing to do things their way or the old way. The same people who excel at running things day to day might not be the ones who are best for changing things.

Once you have the right people in the right seats, it's time to look at your systems. Yes, I mean those association management systems that are baked into so many association cultures—as well as other tools you've been relying on for years. AIIM's Winton notes that when she made the decision to expand content delivery and work to nurture the growing non-member community, she knew the association needed a way to harvest the data that could be coming in from readers, viewers and downloaders. The association invested in HubSpot, a marketing automation tool. "To date, I can say it's been our best investment ever," Winton says.

That's quite a statement. But over the last five years, AIIM has shifted so that more and more of its business is being run through the HubSpot platform—today, Winton says, probably 90 percent of the association's processes use the marketing platform. Webinars are run through HubSpot pages, as are downloads of research papers. AIIM uses the software to track and nurture leads.

As I talked about in Chapter 8, when content is a key part of your business, reusing it is

> If you do not have diverse perspectives on your team, your organization will not be relevant in our changing world.

critical to keep costs down and distribution effective. For every piece of content AIIM creates, it gets around five additional uses, Winton says—a goal that most organizations can shoot for. In AIIM's case, when a report is created, paid members may receive the report in its entirety, as well as the raw underlying data and a slide deck. Meanwhile, the organization will create a one-page executive summary, an infographic and a webinar that are available to everyone, plus dozens, or even hundreds of social posts. In some cases, the organization will also create local events that subscribers can pay to attend. Your exact mix will depend on your distribution model.

For Winton, using a comprehensive marketing product was a natural part of the transition to a marketing-first mindset: "You are the hub," she says. "If our community is where we see the value, why wouldn't we choose a system that would help us optimize the value? It sure as heck isn't an association management system."

Plus, Winton adds, a more streamlined, digitally based system has allowed her to cut costs in other, tangentially related ways. The association completely cut ties to its old office space, instead using drop-in space when necessary. As a result, it's paying 14 percent of what it used to for rent. "We are victims of outdated business models," Winton says. "We need to think differently."

Drive With Data

We all know that data matters. But how do you know which data points to make the focus of your time and resources?

We've all heard about big data—the reams of data points that are supposed to be changing how everyone does business. The problem with the idea of big data is that a resource-limited association can become so focused on collecting and analyzing terabytes of big data that it doesn't have time to figure out what it all really means.

I suggest drilling down a bit, on small- and medium-sized data. The idea is that once you have the pages and pages of data, don't spend hours upon hours trying to sift through and understand it. Instead, have an

Content re-use/atomization

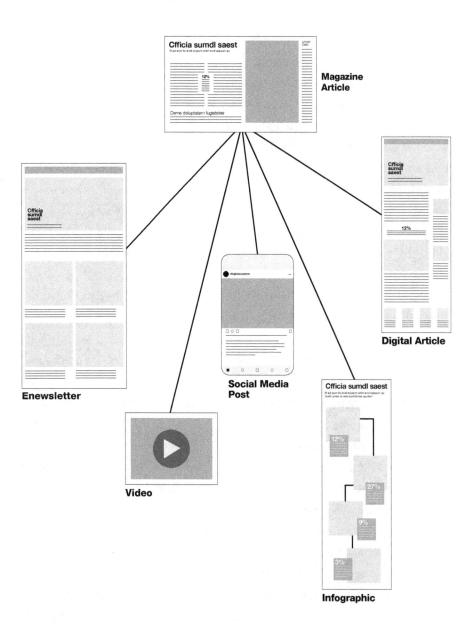

Magazine Article

Digital Article

Enewsletter

Social Media Post

Video

Infographic

idea of what you're looking for first. Then chop up your big data into smaller chunks that break out the trend lines you're looking for. Ignore the rest! It will only take you down a series of rabbit holes that may or may not be fruitful.

Consider Winton's experience at AIIM. Because of a relentless focus on data—the kind that's not searching for a needle in a haystack, but rather based on an insight or trend—she saw, a decade ago, that the value of non-dues-payers was significantly higher than the typical dues-paying members that most associations chase. The nonmembers were the ones who were coming back for different products and services, the ones who had an active need for a solution. That insight triggered the association to shift its business model to one built around monetizing that broader community rather than one focused on collecting members' dues.

Data analysis is particularly important as you begin to make strategic shifts in your marketing and program delivery. Once you've mastered efficient delivery, you must prove the investment was worth it. That's all about small and medium-sized data—those critical key performance indicators that give you a barometer of success. Installing measurement tools—tools that tie membership engagement and action to financial return, like Google Analytics or Adobe Analytics—can help take the rest of your association's leadership from agnostics to advocates.

But again, trying to sift through every data point a tool spits out is a recipe for head-spinning confusion. For meaningful data, decide at the outset which data points are critical to determine your program's success. Are you looking for click-throughs? Qualified leads? Something that feels hard to measure, like thought leadership? There are ways to measure just about everything. For example, Imagination has created a new tool called the Thought Leadership Index, which measures and assesses thought leadership achievement using five crucial data sets to determine whether you're achieving thought leadership success with your target audience.

Knowing which data to look for can help immensely with large-scale changes to your organization. The Project Management Institute (PMI)

How data viz can work

Turn this

Into this

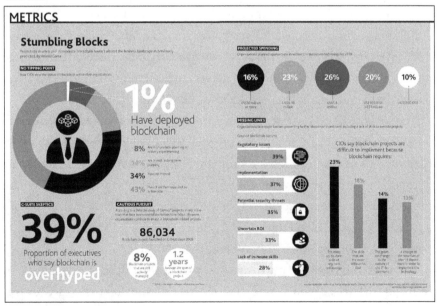

is looking at how its members and prospective members interact across a variety of touchpoints. Leadership can break out the data so they can see that early career members might take a certain course or buy a certain book, while those who are further along in their careers have different behaviors. Knowing those touchpoints helps PMI make the value proposition more meaningful for its key audiences. The marketing mindset touches every interaction: meeting the needs of the customer in a more meaningful way.

Take the time to consider what data you want *before* you begin any program or initiative. Your marketing team should be spending a big chunk of their time on this—and outsourcing it when they could use a hand. Marketers should be adept at basic measurement indicators like A/B testing for everything from headlines to images. At ESA, David Gammel says, the marketing team creates as many as a dozen versions of emails and other communications, tailoring them to specific subdisciplines, past meeting attendance or a host of other criteria.

For many association leaders, getting comfortable with data means making a few strategic hires who can lead that initiative. It's an area where many CEOs simply don't have on-the-ground experience. In a world that's increasingly specialized, that's to be expected.

Use tools to help. Data management and analysis tools have come way down in price and can be stunningly effective in helping you make sense of the reams of data you have coming in. Google Analytics is of course one of them, but it's certainly not the only one. Dashboard tools like Tableau are another useful category: web-based programs that take your spreadsheets, sales data, cloud data, practically anything and transform it into digestible, even beautiful, data visualizations.

You need the right people to oversee your tools. Fill in your own practical gaps with those who can partner with you—and don't expect your legacy in-house techies to have all of the answers. In today's environment, "I have to be willing to hire more professional subject matter experts and get the hell out of the way," says O'Neil.

Step 1
Hire subject matter experts

Step 2
Get the hell out of the way

Get the Board on Board

So, you're ready to start making some changes. It's pretty unlikely that your transformation can be successful without support from your board of directors. Ultimately, your success is the board's success—but that doesn't mean all boards are ready to implement big changes to the way things have been done for years or even decades.

The best place to start is with a policy of frankness. Steen recalls that when he took the helm at American Forests, the board was operating largely in the dark. While they had some idea that things weren't good, the board didn't know just how dire the organization's finances had become. When Steen approached the board to let them know that membership numbers were wildly inflated and revenue figures were presented in a way that was less than transparent, the members of the board were supportive. "My advice in partnering with the board is to always tell the truth," he says. Because he did—even when it wasn't pretty—"I feel like I had the board's support and trust from the beginning," he says.

Association leaders who have been through change suggest being clear and deliberate. If you're working on a large-scale initiative, explain it to the board—then explain that the plan is likely to change once you get going, suggests ESA's Gammel. You want to set up a plan so that you have the freedom to iterate as you move through the process. "One thing you can do," Gammel says, "is talk about a range." For instance, if a certain pot of money is available but you can't be prescriptive on how it'll be spent, request flexibility, explain how you'll iterate through the process, and then note that you may need to come back and ask for more.

The specifics of how you work with your board on big changes will certainly differ depending on the organization and discipline. But in a change-intensive period, board members must be comfortable with a certain amount of gray. That can be tough for board members who see themselves, first and foremost, as stewards of a practice or profession.

It helps, too, to constantly remind yourself of the commitment your board members have made. Never forget that these are volunteer leaders, some of them donating as many as 20 hours a week of their busy lives. They're passionate. They want the best for the future of the profession. Working effectively together means working with them to face the future as effectively as possible.

Over-communication is almost always better in the long run. By no means does that mean including the board in your business decisions. Rather, it means having a good, open relationship and setting expectations on an ongoing basis to avoid any unhappy surprises. "You need some kind of bedrock that's squishy," Gammel says. "Something that gives some direction. Then you can be iterative off of that."

Introducing a three-year or five-year plan to the board is one way to give some clarity even in a sea of gray. The governance structure of an association simply isn't designed to make quick, nimble moves. The more you can engender your board to trust you—with communication, planning and information—the more successful you're going to be. "They're built to be deliberative," says MCI Group's Erin Fuller.

If you're talking about making fundamental changes to membership models—or any other major change—there's no question you'll need to take on an educational role with your board. But a long-term plan is something a board can hold onto—it's a north star, a guiding light. That way, even as board members change, plans can continue without interruption, because the new board members are simply continuing to shepherd a plan down a path. After all, boards change. Hopefully, they change more often than the CEO role does. In five years your board may have turned over completely, but if you apply the things you've read in this book, I'm betting you'll still be in your chair.

Conclu

sion

started writing this book by asking myself and an array
of association leaders what associations are good for. The
standby answer, in some form or another, was content, community and career development. Over the course of writing,
though, I discovered that the associations that are thriving
are good for a lot more than that.

Associations that are growing, associations with a vibrant,
loyal membership or customer base, have long since evolved from that
core understanding of what an association does—they've in essence
changed the definitions of content, community and career. The associations that are excited about the future are the ones that have made
themselves and their offerings essential to the lives of their members.
They see themselves as leaders, as shepherds of a profession or industry.
They are out in front of the big, critical issues that matter most for their
audiences.

The ones that matter are not afraid of the future. They're not scram-
bling to catch up. They're taking a stand, making waves, growing their
tent.

If this doesn't describe your association, it's time to make a change. For
a long time, your members' loyalty probably obscured any weaknesses in

your organization. If your products were a little tired, or your membership pricing off-base, you may not have realized—until recently.

Loyalty no longer provides a cover. Audiences are ruthless about where they spend their dollars and their time.

The truth is, those workaday issues around membership pricing and product suites—the ones that consume so much of many association leaders' energy—are a microcosm of something much larger, of an association industry that is in the midst of a fundamental rethinking of its own worth in an era of fractured attention. Think about it: Does your association matter? Does it really, truly matter? Your association isn't worth much to anyone if it doesn't matter.

Everything you do should have that goal—to matter. To be essential.

The future isn't just about product refreshes and new membership structures. None of that makes a difference if your association doesn't matter—not to the constituents you're trying to serve and not to the broader public. In other words, worry less about disrupting your annual conference agenda and more about disrupting what you stand for and how you communicate that message.

Winning associations still produce content. They provide connections. They hold conferences. But they wrap those core competencies in something much larger: an unwavering commitment to being essential to their members. If you're going to grow and thrive, you must be essential. You must become interwoven in the lives and the livelihoods of your members.

Start by figuring out what the value is that you can bring. What does the profession need? What is its role in the world?

That means:

- Be what the world needs you to be. Stake out your ground. Become the association that's taking a stand on the future of science, the impact of global epidemics, the obesity crisis—whatever matters most.
- Don't just talk about your profession's problems—try to solve them. Whether it's a funding shortage or a public perception problem, associations must be part of the solution.

- Lead the conversation; don't follow it.

Your members may not be asking for this. Real change may be a little uncomfortable. This is not about slapping on a fresh coat of paint and declaring victory.

Done right, this change will make you essential, not just to your members, but to the world.

Source

1. https://www.thepowerofa.org/wp-content/uploads/2012/03/Powerof Associations-2015.pdf
2. http://www.drglennwilson.com/Infomania_experiment_for_HP.doc
3. https://www.theguardian.com/money/2009/oct/05/avoid-multitasking
4. http://time.com/3858309/attention-spans-goldfish/
5. http://money.cnn.com/2010/12/03/news/economy/employers_doing_more_with_less/index.htm
6. https://www.npr.org/2017/07/05/535626109/the-end-of-loyalty-and-the-decline-of-good-jobs-in-america
7. https://rockresearch.com/disrupting-the-traditional-association-membership-model/
8. https://www.edelman.com/trust-barometer
9. https://www.edelman.com/post/america-in-crisis
10. https://www.edelman.com/sites/default/files/2018-04/Edelman_Trust_Barometer_Implications_for_CEOs_2018.pdf
11. https://www.wsj.com/articles/google-vs-google-how-nonstop-political-arguments-rule-its-workplace-1525190574
12. https://www.wsj.com/articles/walmart-takes-a-stand-on-guns-gay-rights-to-get-people-to-like-it-more-1530805106
13. https://www.gmaonline.org/issues-policy/health-nutrition/facts-up-front-front-of-pack-labeling-initiative/
14. http://www.csae.com/About/A-History-of-Associations
15. https://www.ama-assn.org/ama-history
16. https://www.americanbar.org/about_the_aba/
17. http://www.csae.com/About/A-History-of-Associations
18. http://prospect.org/article/associations-without-members
19. https://techcrunch.com/2017/05/02/new-tech-trade-associations-will-have-big-role-in-future-tech-policy/
20. https://www.crunchbase.com/organization/photo-marketing-association-international
21. https://www.nytimes.com/2017/04/18/opinion/how-to-leave-a-mark-on-people.html

22. https://www.nytimes.com/2018/05/28/opinion/failure-educated-elite.
    html?action=click&pgtype=Homepage&clickSource=story-heading&
    module=opinion-c-col-left-region&region=opinion-c-col-left-region&
    WT.nav=opinion-c-col-left-region
23. https://ssir.org/articles/entry/the_secret_of_scale
24. https://associationsnow.com/2015/10/monthly-membership-as-easy-
    as-possible/
25. https://www.asaecenter.org/resources/articles/an_magazine/
    2013/september-october/associations-embrace-new-membership-
    models
26. https://associationsnow.com/2018/02/going-global-growing-
    membership-institute-management-accountants/
27. https://www.financial-planning.com/news/women-cfps-hit-record
28. https://www.fastcompany.com/40477211/as-millennials-demand-
    more-meaning-older-brands-are-not-aging-well
29. http://www.pewresearch.org/fact-tank/2014/04/18/generational-
    equity-and-the-next-america/
30. https://www.cnbc.com/2017/07/21/comscore-ceo-millennials-need-5-
    to-6-second-ads-to-hold-attention.html
31. https://www.prnewswire.com/news-releases/new-ads-from-cfp-
    board-certified--qualified-300224643.html
32. https://www.maa.org/news/american-mathematical-society-and-
    mathematical-association-of-america-announce-ams-acquisition-of
33. https://www.entsoc.org/esa-oxford-university-press-publishing-
    partnership-background-and-frequently-asked-questions
34. https://www.nytimes.com/2018/03/23/business/dealbook/goldman-
    sachs-talk-show.html
35. http://www.hvedc.com/news/foursquare-co-founder-dennis-crowley-
    explains-disruptive-trends-announces-exploratory-efforts-into-
    possible-hudson-valley-office/
36. https://www.southernliving.com/culture/selling-girl-scout-cookies-
    history

37. https://medium.com/@GaryShapiro/cea-is-now-the-consumer-technology-association-9f4a37791ad7
38. https://associationsnow.com/2014/07/platform-collapses-speakers-group-scraps-name-change-after-outcry/
39. https://www.hubspot.com/customers/american-association-of-sleep-technologists
40. https://x.company
41. https://www.ted.com/talks/astro_teller_the_unexpected_benefit_of_celebrating_failure

Index

CPSIA information can be obtained
at www.ICGtesting.com
Printed in the USA
JSHW012002251019
2070JS00001B/1